The Dow Jones-Irwin
Guide to
Put and Call Options

The Dow Jones-Irwin Guide to
Put and Call Options

Henry K. Clasing, Jr.

Dow Jones-Irwin Homewood, Illinois 60430

First Printing, June 1975

Second Printing, October 1975

Third Printing, January 1976

ISBN 0-87094-102-X

Library of Congress Catalog Card No. 74-29746

Printed in the United States of America

To Jean
Who Kept My Dreams Alive

Foreword

The advent of a new type of option has brought about a new era in stock market investing. This new option, created by the Chicago Board Options Exchange, provides for a secondary market—an auction market where every trade is visible. The secondary market in options no longer leaves an investor defenseless against erratic price changes. Whether he is a buyer or a writer, he now has the means to hedge his investment. Henry Clasing deals with this phenomenon clearly and succinctly.

As this becomes apparent to more and more investors, this new option market must find its place as a key money management tool in every equity portfolio.

Until this date I have not been aware of any thorough treatment of this subject in a manner which makes it understandable to the average investor. I believe Mr. Clasing has accomplished this; however, since this market is so young, one must read this book as a *continuing* form of education. Mr. Clasing has attempted to deal with this important fact by showing the dynamics of this investment tool.

I am sure we will hear further from this gifted young man.

LEON POMERANCE
Donaldson, Lufkin & Jenrette
New York, N.Y.

Preface

This book was written for the serious and patient investor who is willing to devote time and energy toward achieving above-average long-term investment success. Its purpose is to explain in detail how stock options are traded. Particular emphasis is given to the structure and operation of the new options exchanges. My major theme is that trading options can be integrated into a prudent overall investment strategy.

This book differs from other books written on the subject of options in several ways. The most significant difference is the explanation of several alternative strategies based on different risk/reward objectives. I have devoted an entire chapter to those tangential aspects of investment management that often prescribe what strategy prevails: taxes and credit. A great deal of effort has been made to illustrate concepts through tables and graphs. After reading this book, the reader will have a sound set of rules to use when trading options.

The greatest amount of thanks for help in creating this book must go to Leon Pomerance. In helping to make this book a competent treatment of the subject he has given the most valu-

able gift anyone can offer, his precious time.
Joseph Gahtan gave me the basic logic he used
when quoting over-the-counter options for many
years. His recommendations helped me immensely in designing the Risk Scoring Method
for quoting OTC options found in the appendix.
Neil Boyle must be given credit for teaching me
his own special techniques for Spreading which,
through his combination of accounting background, trading skill, and expertise in decision
making, have been developed to a fine art. Many
thanks are due to my wife, Jean. She offered
many helpful comments along the way as well
as demonstrating extreme patience for the many
months I spent as a reclusive writer. Producing
a finished product is not an easy job, but Hildegard Vetter and Sara Cowen gave many long
hours at the typewriter keyboard, helping
through corrections and revisions until the job
was complete. They deserve many thanks.

HENRY K. CLASING
May 1975

Contents

List of Figures

List of Tables

Introduction

S tock options have survived many ups and downs throughout history. The typical historical narrative mentions the origin of options as a security in relation to the tulipomania of 17th-century Holland when family fortunes were squandered speculating on the ever-rising prices of tulip bulbs. Later, they were associated with corporate raids to take over railroads in the 19th century United States or with trust building in the 1920s. They were once outlawed in England after the collapse of the South Sea Bubble and were almost prohibited in 1934 during the congressional investigations which followed the Great Crash of 1929. These were the developments that made headlines, but, behind the scenes, a small group of people known as option writers quietly made consistent profits interrupted by an occasional bear market. The important fact to remember is that despite all the controversy options survived.

Now, options have been given a new vitality. Five years ago a small number of option professionals conceived a new idea, the fungible option. If they could create an option that was standardized enough in terms of exercise prices and expiration dates and combine it with a clearing corporation which could act as guarantor, options would take on a whole new dimension. Instead of a one-on-one relationship between a buyer and seller as in the old put and call options they placed the clearing corporation in the middle to break the direct link. The result was the creation of an aftermarket for the new options which introduced tremendous flexibility in terms of the investor's ability to establish or close out his positions.

The more one understands about the structure of the new options exchanges, their ground rules for operation and the type of underlying stocks involved, the more the insight of these pioneers is appreciated. These are truly wise men. They knew the tricks and loopholes well enough to design a vehicle which is not easily tampered with. Most of the designers spent their entire careers dealing with options, and they are committed to giving the new options a long life. In the early stages, as several speculative abuses began to surface, the exchange guidelines for trading were adjusted to eliminate the problem almost as soon as it occurred. In fact, the Securities and Exchange Commission, which is normally dubious about stock brokers' willingness to police themselves, has been pleasantly surprised with the manner in which potential problems have been snuffed out by the industry leaders.

Occasionally a magazine article will call the new options exchanges a gambling casino.[1] It is

[1] Andrew Tobias, "Everyone's Buying Options—but does the S.E.C.?", *New York Magazine*, April 29, 1974.

hoped that the reader will find after reading this book that, in a world where nearly everything is a gamble, at least the new options offer many avenues to handle the odds and much more so than a traditional stock exchange. If a stock is purchased, there is only one direction for the price to move to realize a profit, up. Yet this book will introduce several strategies that yield a substantial profit even if a stock moves 10 percent above *or below* the price at which a stock is purchased. Even with the riskiest option strategy, buying an option, the investor can lose no more than he paid for the option, which might be several hundred dollars. But, for this he is given a reasonable chance to double or triple his money over a short period of time. Even in the best bull markets less than one stock in five doubles in two years. And if a mistake is made in buying a stock, several hundred dollars might not even cover the commissions and taxes.

To understand options one must realize that they are mainly a substitute means of dealing with the underlying stock. This means that, to be successful with options, one must also be able to successfully invest in stocks, except for one major difference. Many option strategies offer much more latitude in terms of how a profit can be made. For example, a profit can be made writing a call if the stock remains at the same price, drops in price, or rises in price less than the amount of the option premium by the end of the option's life.

Every now and then a magazine article or a book is written which tells of a fortune made with options as if it were readily available to anyone.[2] This is a cruel promise. What the author usually doesn't say is that the experience happened once, almost by accident, and hasn't happened again. When a bull market occurs and the headlines are packed with tales of fortunes being made, it is tempting to think that with a little money and a small investment of time, the reader can do the same. This is the first step towards trouble. Whether in 17-century Holland or in the United States of the late 1920s, the trouble began when people began to leave worthwhile pursuits in order to gamble their life savings on becoming rich.[3] And it wasn't just simple folk. The most intelligent, well-to-do people were duped. One of the lessons of history is that when the public begins to believe they have discovered a new way of investing to get rich quick, a certain class of scoundrel will gladly accomodate them and lose their money. In 1929, the vehicle was the leveraged investment trust. And the reason people were so financially destroyed after the Great Crash was that they borrowed even more money after the initial drop in order to recoup their losses. The steady erosion of stock prices into 1932 just finished them off.

The important lessons to learn from history are that it is consistency and good money management that counts. Bernard Baruch had to lose a carriage he gave his wife as a present before

[2] Elizabeth Fowler, *Ninety Days to Fortune* (New York: Ivan Oblensky, 1964).

[3] Charles MacKay, *Extraordinary Popular Delusions and the Madness of Crowds* (New York: Noonday Press, 1932).

he stopped risking all his capital on an investing idea. He also learned to think for himself and not to blindly follow the ideas of others, no matter how powerful or influential they might be. His greatest success came after he opened his own office strictly for himself and operated as a "lone wolf," as he called it.

This book has been designed to permit an interested reader to become a self-sufficient investor in options. He is given the basic option strategies along with a description of the skills needed to be successful. He is presented with a set of sound rules to wisely manage his capital according to the strategy he employs. It is hoped that he will learn to follow the soundness of his own ideas rather than the follies of the market crowd around him. If he follows these guidelines and does his investing homework, while he may not have an easy path to riches, he at least should possess the best chance for success.

The Fungible Option

2

The Chicago Board Options Exchange has launched a new era in stock market investing. By introducing the fungible[1] option they have not only provided a new money management tool in and of itself, but they have elevated investing in common stocks to a new level of sophistication. Just as man progressed from out of the cave to far more protection against the storms of nature, the fungible option provides protection against the vagaries of price disturbances. But, although this new type of option possesses many positive characteristics by itself, it needs many supporting tools in order to produce the profits that are possible to attain. Timing can be a factor of utmost importance, how to measure option premiums another, the relationship between the change in option premiums with the underlying stock still another. To many these are esoteric subjects. They provide a great area for mathematicans to develop measuring devices. What this book will attempt is to offer the reader a down-to-earth approach to these important matters. While the techniques developed

---

[1] As will be seen in the discussion that follows, *fungible* means "mutually interchangeable."

can be applied to stock market investing in general, they are particularly important for success in investing with options. They are the heart of the book.

Before I describe these methods and how to use them, my first order of business will be to provide the necessary background in terms of definitions and the operation of an options exchange, in this case the Chicago Board Options Exchange. While there may be some differences between it and the American Stock Exchange and PBW versions, the CBOE is the pilot model which has shown the way for its followers. The outcome of the growth of the new exchanges will be one clearing corporation for all options, standard terms for the options traded, and uniform margin and trading rules. The one difference will be that the PBW and American Stock Exchange trading will employ the standard specialist system currently employed by the New York Stock Exchange in its stock transactions. The CBOE is unique in its use of board brokers executing public orders coupled with market makers executing their own orders plus directed orders. This feature will be more fully explained later in the chapter.

The fungibility attribute was achieved mainly through the design of a clearing corporation which acts as a guarantor of all options traded. By seeing to it that all contracts are honored, the clearing corporation provides a means to resell a purchased option to another buyer through the clearing corporation mechanism. Likewise, a seller can repurchase an identical option and thus terminate or close out his obligation. This is permissible because the option contracts traded are standardized in terms of the underlying stock, the expiration dates of the options, and the strike prices. What this can mean in terms of strategies will be covered later, but first the basic definitions and terms for this new field. They are extracted from the Chicago Board Clearing Corporation prospectus dated April 26, 1974.

Chicago Board Option ("Option"). A call option traded on the Exchange, which gives the holder the right to buy the number of shares of underlying stock covered by the option from the Clearing Corporation at a stated exercise price prior to a stated expiration date. The designation of a Chicago board option includes the underlying stock, the expiration month and the exercise price (e.g., "XYZ July 50"). A put option, when traded, will offer the right to *sell* 100 shares of the underlying stock at the exercise price prior to the expiration date.

Over-the-Counter Option. A put or call option which may be purchased or sold in the put and call over-the-counter market which existed prior to the formation of the Exchange.

Underlying Stock. The shares of stock subject to being purchased upon the exercise of an option.

Unit of Trading. The number of shares of the underlying stock designated by the Exchange as the subject of a single option contract. In the absence of any other designation, the unit of trading is 100 shares.

Exercise Price. The price per share at which the holder of the option may purchase the underlying stock upon exercise. The exercise price is sometimes called the "striking price."

Expiration Date. The last day on which an option may be exercised. Since commencing operations, the Exchange has made a change in the time options expire, effective with respect to options expiring in July 1974 and thereafter. In order to exercise options expiring in July 1974 and thereafter, an exercise notice must be received *at the Clearing Corporation* no later than 10:30 A.M. Chicago time on the last Monday of the expiration month (or, if the last Monday is a holiday on which there is no Exchange trading, on the next business day). Holders of options should determine from their brokers the time limit for instructing the broker to exercise an option, so that the expiration deadline at the Clearing Corporation may be met.

Premium. The aggregate price of the option agreed upon between the buyer and writer or their agents in a transaction on the floor of the Exchange.

Opening Purchase Transaction. A transaction in which an investor intends to become the holder of an option.

Opening Sale Transaction. A transaction in which an investor intends to become the writer of an option.

Closing Purchase Transaction. A transaction in which an investor who has previously written an option liquidates his position as a writer. This is accomplished by "purchasing" in a closing purchase transaction on the Exchange an option having the same terms as the option previously written. Such a transaction has the effect of cancelling the investor's preexisting position as a writer, instead of resulting in the issuance of an option to the investor.

Closing Sale Transaction.   A transaction in which an investor who has previously purchased an option liquidates his position as a holder. This is accomplished by "selling" in a closing sale transaction an option having the same terms as the option previously purchased. Such a transaction has the effect of liquidating the investor's preexisting position as a holder of the option, instead of resulting in the investor's assuming the obligation of a writer.

Covered Writer.   A writer of an option who, so long as he remains a writer, owns the underlying stock covered by the option, or owns a call in the same underlying stock.

Uncovered Writer.   A writer of an option who is not a covered writer.

The Clearing Corporation mentioned in the above definitions is an integral part of the exchange mechanism and a feature which offers great advantages over the OTC option market. The CBOE Clearing Corporation is the obligor of all the options traded in the CBOE auction market. The Clearing Corporation handles the accounting of the option trades between members of the Exchange, supervises the capital requirements of its members, and issues the exercise notices to its members when options are exercised; the members are then obliged to assign the exercise notices on a consistent basis to their customers. This procedure removes the one-on-one linkage between an individual buyer of an option and an individual writer which characterizes the OTC market. (Breaking this direct linkage between buyer and seller avoids the often sticky problem of a seller's wanting a buyer to exercise, but the buyer's refusing, even if it is to his advantage. Where the seller wanted the opportunity to unwind a position and open a new one, he was often frustrated. Worse yet, if the underlying stock began a sharp decline and the writer wanted to back out of his obligation, he couldn't. He was locked in.)

Another important Clearing Corporation feature is the collective backing of all option contracts by the CBOE members. Besides the minimum capital requirements of $150,000 or 8⅓ percent of its aggregate indebtedness, whichever is greater, each member must contribute an initial deposit of $10,000 to a clearing fund. This deposit is increased each quarter if necessary to maintain it at a level of $10 times the average daily number of open option positions. In case a member firm fails to discharge an obligation rising from a trade on the CBOE within 24 hours, his deposit is applied to discharge the obligation. If this deposit is insufficient to cover the amount, all remaining members are charged for the still outstanding amount on a pro-rata basis. If their Clearing Fund deposits are reduced because of this assessment, they must be promptly brought back to the required level. In addition, every option traded is fully margined by 9 A.M. the next morning. (By contrast, an OTC option is merely guaranteed by the New York Stock Exchange member who has handled the writer's side of the transaction. If he defaults, the firm should make good on the contract. But, if the firm goes into bankruptcy, the buyer may get only partial fulfillment of the contract, and then only after lengthy legal proceedings. Because of this arrangement, experienced option traders pay particular attention during precarious stock market conditions to the identity of the firm on the other side of their option transactions.)

The proof of the CBOE's superiority to the OTC option market is the fact that all OTC trading in calls also traded on the CBOE virtually disappeared the moment CBOE trading began. The CBOE began operation on April 26, 1973, trading exclusively in call options for 16 underlying stocks Put options may be traded as well by the end of 1975, but, since the demand for puts is far less than that for calls, the obvious choice was to begin trading in calls. The underlying stocks which qualify for options trading on the CBOE must conform to the following qualifications: (*a*) they must have a minimum of 10,000,000 shares outstanding at least 8,000,-000 of which are (according to reports filed with the SEC) beneficially owned by persons other than officers or directors of the issuer or 10 percent stockholders; (*b*) trading volume on the principal securities exchange on which the stock is listed of at least 1,000,000 shares per year in each of the two previous calendar years; and (c) a market price of at least $10 per share.

Less than 200 stocks can pass these strict guidelines, and all of them are listed on the New York Stock Exchange. Besides the requirement that all companies so qualifying conform to all SEC reporting regulations, each company must meet the following requirements:

1. A majority of the existing board of directors of the issuer have been directors of the issuer or a predecessor of the issuer from the beginning of the issuer's last three fiscal years;

2. the issuer and its subsidiaries have not during the past ten years defaulted in the payment of any dividend or sinking fund installment on preferred stock, or in the payment of any principal, interest, or sinking fund installment on any indebtedness for borrowed money, or in the payment of rentals under long-term leases;

3. the issuer and its consolidated subsidiaries had a net income, after taxes but before extraordinary items net of tax effect, of at least $500,000 for each of the last five fiscal years;

4. the issuer earned in each of the last five fiscal years any dividends, including the fair market value of any stock dividends, paid in each such year on all classes of securities.

The CBOE may make exceptions to one or more of the above requirements, or may continue to trade in options of the underlying stocks even though the issuer might fail in the future to meet these requirements. These stringent listing requirements are also in sharp contrast to OTC options. Because a buyer of an OTC call has to attain a price move in the underlying stock equal to the premium he paid just to break even he has a bias to deal in the most volatile, speculative stocks he can find. For this reason OTC call writers are forced to deal in these potentially troublesome issues. The CBOE, by dealing in the most widely held stocks and by providing the liquidity of its aftermarket, allows both writer and buyer to deal in issues least likely to incur unpleasant fundamental surprises.

As of July 1, 1974, the CBOE was trading call options in the 32 common stocks listed in Table 2–1.

The yield of each stock is included to demonstrate another important feature of CBOE calls, the writer's claim to all stock dividends. If a call is exercised on the CBOE, the buyer takes delivery of the stock free of any dividends declared during the life of the call. This makes a great deal of sense, since the writer has the orientation of making a certain return on his capital, which is usually tied up in the stock used to guarantee the calls he writes. While the average yield was below the yield of the Dow Jones Industrial Average, 3.6 for CBOE versus 5.7 for the DJIA as of July 1, 1974, there were a number of stocks such as American Telephone, Exxon, Ford, INA, IT&T, International Harvester, and Loews Corporation which yielded in excess of 6 percent.

TABLE 2–1

Underlying Stocks on the CBOE as of July, 1974

Stock	*Yield (percent)*
American Telephone & Telegraph	6.7
Atlantic Richfield	2.2
Avon Products	3.1
Bethlehem Steel	5.3
Brunswick	2.4
Citicorp	2.6
Eastman Kodak	1.5
Exxon	6.5
Ford	6.5
Gulf & Western	3.6
Great Western Financial	3.6
IBM	2.8
INA	6.1
IT&T	7.0
Internatl. Harvester	6.4
Kerr McKee	1.1
Kresge	0.7
Loews Corp.	7.6
McDonalds Corp.	—
Merck	1.8
Minnesota Mining	1.7
Monsanto	3.8
Northwest Airlines	2.0
Pennzoil	5.6
Polaroid	0.9
RCA	6.5
Sears Roebuck	1.9
Sperry Rand	2.0
Texas Instruments	1.1
Upjohn	1.3
Weyerhaeuser	2.1
Xerox	0.9
Average Yield	3.6

The OTC option market, surprisingly, has a dividend rule exactly opposite to the CBOE. Upon exercise, the OTC buyer takes delivery of his stock with all dividend rights incurred during the option period.

At the beginning of the chapter it was mentioned that the CBOE had created an aftermarket for their options by standardizing the strike prices and expiration dates of their options. This was accomplished by establishing the end of January, April, July, and October as standard expiration dates. At any one point in time there are three outstanding time periods, so that, as of February 1, there would be three-month, six-month and nine-month options trading. As time passes, the time to maturity gradually dwindles until the three-month option expires and a new nine-month option begins trading.

The CBOE option calendar in Table 2–2 details the exact times to maturity for any options outstanding at any point in time. This will be important for our later discussion about option premiums.

The standard strike or exercise prices are determined at five-point intervals for stock prices below 50, at ten-point intervals for stocks trading between 50 and 100 and 20-point intervals for stocks trading above 100. If the stock trades at a new price level falling within the strike price guidelines, a new option will usually begin trading at that level.

Since the key variables describing a CBOE option are its strike price and its expiration date, these elements form the standard label for a

TABLE 2–2

CBOE Option Calendar

Week	Months to Maturity of CBOE Options			
	Jan.	Apr.	July	Oct.
January				
Week 1	1.0	4.0	7.0	—
Week 2	0.8	3.8	6.8	—
Week 3	0.5	3.5	6.5	—
Week 4	0.3	3.3	6.3	—
Week 5	0.2	3.2	6.2	—
February				
Week 1	—	3.0	6.0	9.0
Week 2	—	2.8	5.8	8.8
Week 3	—	2.5	5.5	8.5
Week 4	—	2.3	5.3	8.3
Week 5	—	2.2	5.2	8.2
March				
Week 1	—	2.0	5.0	8.0
Week 2	—	1.8	4.8	7.8
Week 3	—	1.5	4.5	7.5
Week 4	—	1.3	4.3	7.3
Week 5	—	1.2	4.2	7.2
April				
Week 1	—	1.0	4.0	7.0
Week 2	—	0.8	3.8	6.8
Week 3	—	0.5	3.5	6.5
Week 4	—	0.3	3.3	6.3
Week 5	—	0.2	3.2	6.2
May				
Week 1	9.0	—	3.0	6.0
Week 2	8.8	—	2.8	5.8
Week 3	8.5	—	2.5	5.5
Week 4	8.3	—	2.3	5.3
Week 5	8.2	—	2.2	5.2
June				
Week 1	8.0	—	2.0	5.0
Week 2	7.8	—	1.8	4.8
Week 3	7.5	—	1.5	4.5
Week 4	7.3	—	1.3	4.3
Week 5	7.2	—	1.2	4.2
July				
Week 1	7.0	—	1.0	4.0
Week 2	6.8	—	0.8	3.8
Week 3	6.5	—	0.5	3.5

TABLE 2–2 (*continued*)

Week	Jan.	Apr.	July	Oct.
	Months to Maturity of CBOE Options			
Week 4.........	6.3	—	0.3	3.3
Week 5.........	6.2	—	0.2	3.2
August				
Week 1.........	6.0	9.0	—	3.0
Week 2.........	5.8	8.8	—	2.8
Week 3.........	5.5	8.5	—	2.5
Week 4.........	5.3	8.3	—	2.3
Week 5.........	5.2	8.2	—	2.2
September				
Week 1.........	5.0	8.0	—	2.0
Week 2.........	4.8	7.8	—	1.8
Week 3.........	4.5	7.5	—	1.5
Week 4.........	4.3	7.3	—	1.3
Week 5.........	4.2	7.2	—	1.2
October				
Week 1.........	4.0	7.0	—	1.0
Week 2.........	3.8	6.8	—	0.8
Week 3.........	3.5	6.5	—	0.5
Week 4.........	3.3	6.3	—	0.3
Week 5.........	3.2	6.2	—	0.2
November				
Week 1.........	3.0	6.0	9.0	—
Week 2.........	2.8	5.8	8.8	—
Week 3.........	2.5	5.5	8.5	—
Week 4.........	2.3	5.3	8.3	—
Week 5.........	2.2	5.2	8.2	—
December				
Week 1.........	2.0	5.0	8.0	—
Week 2.........	1.8	4.8	7.8	—
Week 3.........	1.5	4.5	7.5	—
Week 4.........	1.3	4.3	7.3	—
Week 5.........	1.2	4.2	7.2	—

given option. An "Atlantic Richfield July 100" designates the underlying stock, the expiration date, and the strike price. The standard newspaper quotes from the *Wall Street Journal* organize this information as shown in Figure 2–1.

FIGURE 2–1

Chicago Board Options Exchange

Monday, July 1, 1974

Closing prices of all options. Sales unit is 100 shares. Security description includes exercise price.

Option &	price	— Jul — Vol.	Last	— Oct — Vol.	Last	— Jan — Vol.	Last	Stock Close
Am Tel	50	368	⅛	130	13-16	81	1 9-16	46
Atl R	90	168	2⅜	40	5½	29	7¾	89⅛
Atl R	100	21	⅜	26	2⅜	b	b	89⅛
Avon ..	90	a	a	b	b	b	b	.....
Avon ...	80	a	a	b	b	b	b	.....
Avon ..	70	a	a	b	b	b	b	
Avon	60	117	⅛	74	1½	b	b	47¼
Avon	50	171	1 5-16	75	3⅞	42	6¼	47¼
Avon	45	148	3¾	39	6¼	43	8⅞	47¼
Beth S	30	79	1¼	61	2⅜	48	3¼	30⅛
Beth S ..	35	87	⅛	34	13-16	24	1⅜	30⅛
Bruns .	20	20	1-16	b	b	b	b	13½
Bruns	15	41	⅜	65	1	25	1⅝	13½
Bruns .	25	a	a	b	b	b	b	.....
Citicp ..	50	a	a	b	b	b	b	.....
Citicp .	45	2	1-16	b	b	b	b	31
Citicp	40	208	⅛	117	9-16	69	1¼	31
Citicp ..	35	b	b	127	1⅝	60	2½	31
Eas Kd	140	62	1-16	b	b	b	b	104¼
Eas Kd	120	146	⅜	57	2⅝	b	b	104¼
Eas Kd	100	237	6¾	79	11	5	14	104¼
Exxon	100	a	a	b	b	b	b	....
Exxon	90	a	a	33	7-16	b	b	70⅜
Exxon	80	71	⅛	63	1⅝	84	3⅛	70⅜
Exxon	70	b	b	89	5	27	6⅞	70⅜
Ford ..	60	74	1-16	b	b	b	b	49⅛
Ford	50	169	1⅛	80	2⅞	33	4⅜	49⅛
Ford ..	45	43	4¾	24	6	b	b	49⅛
Ford	40	27	9⅛	b	b	b	b	49⅛
Glf Wn	25	57	¼	43	1⅛	44	2	22½
Glf Wn	30	2	1-16	b	b	b	b	22½
Gt Wst	20	89	1-16	827	¼	416	½	11
Gt Wst	15	b	b	524	¾	227	1 5-16	11
I B M	270	42	⅛	25	1 9-16	b	b	212¾
I B M	240	284	⅝	100	6½	13	11½	212¾
I B M	220	b	b	58	13¾	29	19¼	212¾
I N A ..	35	a	a	78	¼	b	b	25⅜
I N A ..	40	1	1-16	70	1-16	b	b	25⅜
I N A ..	30	12	⅛	8	⅝	30	1 3-16	25⅜
I T T ..	35	a	a	b	b	b	b	...
I T T ..	30	a	a	23	3-16	b	b	20
I T T ..	25	121	⅛	81	11-16	152	1⅛	20
I T T .	20	120	¾	141	2	111	2⅝	20
In Har	30	59	1-16	119	7-16	b	b	23⅜
In Har	35	1	1-16	b	b	b	b	23⅜
In Har	25	60	½	67	1⅜	64	2⅛	23⅜
Kerr M	65	35	2½	15	5⅛	17	7⅝	64¾
Kerr M	75	126	¼	79	2⅜	b	b	64¾
Kerr M	85	122	1-16	16	⅞	b	b	64¾
Kresge	40	28	3-16	b	b	b	b	33¾
Kresge	35	169	1⅛	89	3¼	27	4⅛	33¾
Kresge	30	62	4¼	1	6⅛	6	7	33¾
Loews	25	a	a	50	⅛	b	b	15⅞
Loews	20	105	⅛	25	½	5	13-16	15⅞
Loews	15	b	b	75	1¾	49	2½	15⅞
M M M	95	a	a	b	b	b	b	....
M M	85	10	⅛	b	b	b	b	72⅜
M M	75	22	1⅝	17	4	2	6⅛	72⅜
Mc Don	60	319	3-16	288	1½	48	2⅝	48⅛
Mc Don	70	51	1-16	b	b	b	b	48⅛
Mc Don	50	425	2	226	4⅜	60	6⅜	48⅛
Merck	90	60	⅛	b	b	b	b	79¼
Merck ..	80	69	2½	16	5½	5	8¼	79¼
Monsan	70	200	⅝	b	b	b	b	63⅞
Monsan	60	88	5⅝	46	8	30	10½	63⅞
Monsan	50	12	14¼	b	b	b	b	63⅞
Nw Air	25	152	9-16	170	2	50	3	22⅝
Nw Air	20	60	3⅜	35	4¾	b	b	22⅝
Pnz U	25	44	1-16	50	7-16	5	¾	17¾
Pnz U	250	34	⅛	37	⅝	b	b	17¾
Pnz U	20	b	b	135	15-16	84	1 13-16	17¾
Polar ..	110	a	a	b	b	b	b	....
Polar ..	95	a	a	b	b	b	b	..
Polar ..	80	a	a	24	⅛	b	b	35⅝
Polar ..	60	112	⅛	19	⅜	81	15-16	35⅝
Polar .	45	b	b	172	1¾	31	3	35⅝
Polar ..	40	b	b	162	3½	111	4⅞	35⅝
R C A .	25	5	1-16	b	b	b	b	15⅜
R C A	20	762	1-16	146	⅜	65	¾	15⅜
R C A	15	b	b	112	1⅜	59	2⅛	15⅜
Sears ..	100	a	a	b	b	b	b	
Sears	90	16	½	49	2⅝	b	b	83¾
Sears ..	80	12	4½	2	7	55	9⅝	83¾
Sperry ..	40	33	⅞	19	2⅞	13	4¼	37⅝
Sperry	45	6	⅛	11	1⅛	b	b	37⅝
Sperry	55	a	a	b	b	b	b	
Tex In	100	314	1 15-16	136	6⅝	11	9¼	93½
Tex In	120	35	⅛	108	1¾	b	b	93½
Upjohn	75	233	4¼	68	8¼	8	11½	75⅝
Upjohn	85	134	⅝	132	3⅞	3	6½	75⅝
Upjohn	100	73	⅛	b	b	b	b	75⅝
Upjohn	65	18	11¾	8	14¾	1	17¼	75⅝
Weyerh	35	46	3⅛	25	4⅜	b	b	37½
Weyerh	40	45	½	28	2⅛	17	3⅛	37½
Weyerh	45	30	⅛	24	13-16	11	1½	37½
Xerox	160	10	1-16	b	b	b	b	115⅝
Xerox	140	34	3-16	b	b	b	b	115⅝
Xerox	120	267	3	73	8½	14	11¾	115⅝

Total volume 16,325. Open interest 380,812. ....

a—Not traded. b—Unavailable.

Courtesy of Dow Jones & Co.

They present the underlying stock with the strike price adjacent to it. Then, in three sets of columns to the right they present the volume in terms of options traded and the closing premium for the near-, mid- and far-term contracts. The closing price for the underlying stock is presented as the last column on the right.

The next logical question should be, how are

the option premiums determined? This subject will be covered completely in the following chapter on pricing the new options.

Once we know how much to pay or obtain in premiums for an option, the next area of investigation should be trading. Again, the CBOE has conceived an excellent design. In order to produce the liquidity which characterizes the CBOE, an ingenious system was devised. It is a hybrid of the New York Stock Exchange specialist system and the over-the-counter securities markets. Rather than having a stock assigned to one specialist, who then supposedly buys and sells stock against the tide of broker orders, the CBOE has a board broker who handles *only* customers' orders. He buys and sells no options for his own account as a New York Stock Exchange specialist would. The CBOE board broker keeps a book of all customer orders for which *no* member firm or market maker orders are entered. The market maker represents the other part of the CBOE hybrid system. He is allowed to buy and sell options for his own account *only*. He can quote his trades within a point range of the board broker, but if he is quoting a premium either on the buy or sell side at the same price as the board broker, the board broker's trades take *priority*. With this set of operating rules the thorny specialist problem has been solved in favor of the individual customer. His orders take priority over the "insiders" or market makers. In a world where many people have grown cynical about the unfairness of the "system," the CBOE has bent over backwards for the individual investor.

How should orders be placed? When an individual has decided that the precise moment has arrived to either buy or sell an option, he is usually best served by obtaining a market quote and then giving himself a $\frac{1}{16}$ point leeway for options trading under $2 ($200 for a 100-share option), $\frac{1}{8}$ leeway above 2 and below 10, and $\frac{1}{4}$ above 10. In other words, if the current bid-offer market quote is $2\frac{1}{2}$ to 3, 1 by 2, this means that there is an order on the floor to buy at $2\frac{1}{2}$ and another to sell at 3. The "1 by 2" tells you that there is one option to buy at $2\frac{1}{2}$ and two options for sale at 3. If you were an anxious buyer, you would place an order to buy at 3 with $\frac{1}{8}$ discretion. This allows your broker on the floor of the exchange to pay $3\frac{1}{8}$ if he has to in order to complete the transaction. If you were an anxious seller instead, your $\frac{1}{8}$ leeway (or "discretion" in auction market terms) would be used relative to the bid of $2\frac{1}{2}$ so that a typical order might be to sell at $2\frac{1}{2}$ with $\frac{1}{8}$ discretion, meaning you will accept $2\frac{3}{8}$ as your price if necessary to complete the trade.

If an investor is more patient or is not reacting to a recent news development, he should use limit orders to be placed on the board broker's book. If an investor has estimated from the behavior of the underlying stock and the premium curves introduced in the next chapter that a given option should trade in the vicinity of $3, he should place either a day order, if he is reevaluating daily, or a G.T.C. (good 'til cancelled) order on the *board broker's book* (this is important) to buy or sell at a price of $3. Option premiums are volatile to the extent that an investor who chases a market—in other words he turns bullish *after* strength occurs in the market—will invariably "pay up" for all his trades. The ideal is to have some estimate of a reasonable price and attempt to trade at that level. To accomplish this requires some trading skill and price measurements. These subjects will be treated in the chapter on price behavior.

In terms of trading, an option that is initially purchased is either resold in the auction market for a profit or a loss, exercised to take delivery of the underlying stock, or allowed to expire worthless. An option initially sold (written) is either repurchased to close out the position, allowed to expire worthless, in which case the premium is realized as a profit, or exercised, in which case the writer must honor the option obligation. Exercising is the term which describes the action of the buyer of a call who decides to take advantage of the contract terms of the call option he owns and take delivery of the optioned stock. For all practical purposes, he will decide to do this only at the end of the call's life. At any time before that he is better off simply selling his call for a profit in the CBOE aftermarket. This is so because he incurs an added brokerage commission on the 100 shares of stock involved in the exercise. If he can cash in his profits on a stock rise before the contract expires by simply reselling his call, why should he incur the added exercise expense, not to mention the capital required to purchase the 100 shares of underlying stock at an earlier date than expiration?

All CBOE call options can be exercised at

any time prior to 10:30 A.M. on the last Monday of the particular expiration month in question. If the last Monday is a holiday, the next business day is designated. To exercise an option, an exercise notice must be tendered to the CBOE Clearing Corporation prior to the deadline just stated. This notice can be tendered only by the clearing member in whose account the option is held, and only in a form acceptable to the Clearing Corporation. If a certificate has been issued evidencing an option (this is exceptional and probably occurs only if an account has been transferred from one broker to another and proof of option ownership has been requested), this certificate should accompany the exercise notice. To be completely safe an investor should check with his broker for the broker's own deadline, which may be somewhat earlier than the CBOE's. All trading in expiring options ceases at 2:00 P.M. Chicago time on the business day prior to the expiration date. An investor should be very careful about respecting these dates, because the only way he can realize the potential profit in a purchased call is by exercising after trading ceases at 2:00 P.M. on the day prior to the expiration date. When an exercise notice is tendered to the CBOE Clearing Corporation, it is randomly assigned by computer to a Clearing Member who has an account with the Clearing Corporation reflecting an option or options of the same denomination being exercised. The Clearing Member then assigns the exercise notice on some consistent selection basis, whether random, "first in, first out," or otherwise. This method must be on record with the

CBOE and can only be changed on approval of the CBOE and through notice to the firm's customers.

The commission rates charged by CBOE members to their customers were determined by the following formulas until April 30, 1975, when all fixed commissions were scheduled to be terminated by the SEC. At that time brokerage commissions will probably be set by one or more industry leaders. The rates prior to April 30, 1975, were as follows:

1. Orders for the purchase, sale, or exercise of a single option:

Money Involved in the Order	*Minimum Commission*
$ 100– 2,499	1.3% + $12
2,500–4,777	0.9% + $22
4,778–29,999	$65

2. Orders for the purchase, sale, or exercise of multiple options:

Money Involved in the Order	*Minimum Commission*
$ 100– 2,499	1.3% + $12
2,500–19,999	0.9% + $22
20,000–29,999	0.6% + $82

Plus:
First to tenth option covered by the order: $6 per option
Eleventh option and over covered by the order: $4 per option

In all cases, however, the minimum commissions on a single option order involving over $100 and under $30,000 can not be less than $25 or more than $65. On single or multiple option orders involving options with premiums of less than $100 each, the commission is *mutually agreed* for those options. On the portion of an order exceeding $30,000 in dollar amount, the commissions are subject to negotiation. For example, in a transaction involving the purchase of an option covering 100 shares of Atlantic Richfield at an exercise price of $100 by individual A from writer B at a premium of $1,200, both A and B must pay their brokers a minimum commission of $27.60 (1.3 percent of $1,200 plus $12), while A pays B $1,200 for the option. If either A or B closed out his transaction in the aftermarket, another minimum commission would be paid his broker based on the dollar amount at that time. If A decided to exercise 100 shares at $100 each, both he and the writer receiving the exercise notice would be required to pay their respective brokers a minimum commission of $65.

Margin requirements are uniform for all the approved options exchanges and are as follows:

1. All purchases of options must be paid for in cash within one business day of the trade. The options have no loan value in a margin account.
2. All opening sales (writing of options) where the underlying stock is owned by the investor require no margin. The only limitation is that when valuing the equity in the account, the equity value of the stock cannot exceed the exercise value of the call written.
3. The uncovered writing of calls is subject to the following rules:

a. The rules are based on the value of the underlying security.

    (1) 30 percent of the value of the underlying security is required. (Some brokers may require as much as 50 percent.)

    (2) Margin is increased or decreased by the amount the option is in or out of the money.

    (3) Minimum margin is $250 per contract.

    (4) The original premium received reduces the initial margin requirement.

EXAMPLE

For an Atlantic Richfield 100-option with a premium of $900 and a price for the underlying stock of 95 the margin would be as follows:

30% times the market value of the underlying stock.......................	$2,850
Less "out of the money" amount.........	−500
Margin Required.....................	$2,350
Less the option premium received........	−900
Additional cash margin needed.......	$1,450

If the stock price moved up ten points to 105, the margin calculation for a "mark to the market" would be as follows:

30% times the market value of the underlying stock.......................	$3,150
Plus "in the money" value...............	+500
Margin Required.....................	$3,650

Note: Where the stock value has appreciated $1,000 the margin requirement increased $1,300 from $2,350 to $3,650 or 130 percent of the increase in the underlying stock's value.

The subject of income tax will be covered briefly for the individual in order to provide the background necessary to understand the examples of strategies presented in the following chapters.

For the purchasing of call options the logic is simply that a call is a capital asset and therefore receives capital gains treatment as follows:

Stock Price Behavior	Tax Treatment*
1. Stock is up, call resold for a profit	Short- or long-term capital gain depending whether call was owned for less or more than six months; e.g., call purchased for $400, sold for $600, three months later becomes a short-term capital gain of $200.
2. Stock is down, call resold at a loss†	Short- or long-term capital loss depending on whether call was held for less or more than six months; e.g., call purchased for $600, sold for $300 seven months later, becomes a long-term capital loss of $300.
3. Stock is down, option expires worthless†	Short- or long-term capital loss depending on whether call was held for less or more than six months; e.g., call purchased for $500, expires worthless in four months for a short-term capital loss of $500.
4. Stock is up, call exercised	The call premium paid is added to the price of the stock to become the cost base for the security. The time period for capital gain or loss calculations for the stock begins upon the exercise of the option; e.g., a call costing $1,000 is exercised at a strike price of $100, producing a cost basis of $110 for the stock.

* In the examples given commissions are not taken into account.
† It is possible to incur a loss in a call with the stock price unchanged simply because of passage of time.

The writing of calls receives an entirely different tax treatment based on an IRS ruling issued to the CBOE during April 1974 which states that any profit or loss incurred in a closing transaction for a written call should receive *ordinary treatment.* This means that such gains or losses are added to or subtracted from any income reported as gross taxable income on an individual's tax form, whether salary, dividends, etc.

The exact treatment for the four possible cases is:

Stock Price Behavior	Tax Treatment*
1. Stock price is up, call repurchased at a loss	Loss on call is an ordinary loss; e.g., a call written at $900 rises to $1,200 where it is repurchased for a $300 ordinary loss.
2. Stock price is up, call is exercised	The call premium is added to the proceeds of the stock obtained upon the exercise, with the total proceeds compared to the cost base of the stock. The time period for capital gain or loss is determined by the holding period of the stock. E.g., a call written at $500 is exercised at a strike price of 50. The sale price becomes 50 plus the call premium or $55. Since the stock was purchased seven months earlier at $40, the result is a long-term capital gain of $1,500.
3. Stock price is down, call repurchased at a gain	The gain on the call is an ordinary gain. E.g., a call written at $900 is repurchased at $500 for a $400 ordinary gain.
4. Stock price is down, call expires worthless	The premium received is treated as ordinary income, realized at the expiration date. E.g., a call written at $500 expires worthless for a $500 ordinary gain realized upon expiration.

* In the examples given, commissions are not taken into the account.

Now that the background regarding the CBOE has been covered the reader should be prepared for the fun part, application, the art and science of making money by the use of options.

Pricing the New Options

3

The ability to price an option is a key ingredient to success with options investing. If an investor can predetermine whether an option premium is above or below a fair economic value based on the important price determinants, he has a decided advantage over his less informed counterpart. If he is a writer he wants the fattest premiums available for several reasons, the primary one being the added profit or protection he will receive relative to his investment. But almost as important is the fact that the overvalued premium gives him an edge. If the premium returns to a more normal valuation during the life of his position, this is an additional source of profit. Other investors will have to depend solely on time and the price behavior of the underlying stock.

If an investor is a buyer, he wants the best buy for his money in terms of what he has to pay to realize a potential profit. Since leverage is important, an option purchased at $200 which rises to $400 yields a profit of 100 percent compared with the same option purchased for $250, which only yields a 60-percent result.

Another tremendous advantage is the ability

to predetermine with a high degree of accuracy what a premium might be if a stock rose ten points in two months or declined 20 points in five months. Many such evaluations can be made before establishing a position in order to decide whether the transaction is worthwhile or not.

To provide such measurements, the top brokerage firms have commissioned consultants and developed expensive computer programs which generate such information. But, since these inputs may not be available to every reader, in order to make him self-sufficient and capable of making his own decisions, this chapter will provide him with all the premium measuring tools he needs. The few computations are relatively simple and the rest merely is a matter of reading premium values from a set of graphs.

The important factors used to evaluate option premiums are all related to the return an option writer can expect as compensation for his tying up capital to honor the option contract and for the risk he undertakes by either owning the optioned stock or placing in reserve the cash to buy the stock for delivery at exercise time, if such an event occurs. The usual variables used to estimate option premiums are the time remaining in the option, the stock's dividend rate and the stock's price volatility as a proxy for risk. The first two variables are simply measured, but volatility is more of a challenge.

Burton Malkiel, author, with Richard Quandt,

of a book on stock options,[1] as well as of the
well-known *A Random Walk Down Wall Street,*
suggests the following measure:

$$\text{Estimated Volatility} = \frac{\text{52-Week Stock Price Range}}{\text{Average 52-Week Stock Price}}$$

Or, in terms of algebra,

$$\text{Estimated Volatility} = \frac{H - L}{(H + L)/2}$$

where

H = the stock's 52-week high
L = the stock's 52-week low

These statistics are readily obtained from the
Media General Financial Weekly, sold at most
financial district newsstands. This book uses a
variation of Malkiel's approach, which seems
to relate more to a commonsense understanding
of stock price behavior. Half the 52-week range
is used instead of the entire range. This may
seem a small difference, but the result is a
volatility measure which estimates the move
that a stock can be expected to have above or
below its average price during a year's time.
For example a 10-percent volatility for American Telephone would suggest a high of 55 for
a year if the average price were expected to be
50. In this manner the volatility of American
Telephone can easily be compared to that of
Polaroid, a 40-percent volatile stock on average,
which would have an estimated high of 70 if the

---

[1] B. G. Malkiel and R. E. Quandt, Strategies and
Rational Decisions in the Securities Options Market
(Cambridge, Mass.: MIT Press, 1969).

average price were expected to be 50. A list of these volatility measures is presented in Table 3–1.

Perhaps surprisingly, the volatility for most stocks is a rather stable measure from year to

TABLE 3–1

Volatility Measures for CBOE Stocks

Stock	1971	1972	1973	52 Weeks Ending July 1, 1974
American Telephone.........	13.9%	13.1%	9.6%	8.6%
Atlantic Richfield..........	15.4	24.4	26.0	17.0
Avon.....................	15.4	34.2	42.0	49.7
Bethlehem Steel............	20.2	15.7	18.3	18.9
Brunswick.................	43.2	35.7	52.3	42.4
Citicorp..................	18.0	28.1	21.0	28.3
Eastman Kodak............	16.3	23.3	18.9	20.4
Exxon....................	10.3	13.5	10.4	17.6
Ford.....................	14.9	13.4	36.2	23.5
Gulf & Western............	24.0	23.0	30.5	22.6
Great Western Financial.....	22.2	20.0	41.1	40.3
IBM......................	12.7	12.5	21.7	22.4
INA......................	24.5	17.4	23.6	30.5
IT&T.....................	19.0	14.4	41.4	39.2
Internatl. Harvester........	19.1	20.4	27.6	23.7
Kerr-McGee...............	21.9	27.4	28.9	28.8
Kresge...................	28.7	22.6	28.0	21.6
Loews Corp................	25.7	16.9	49.4	34.9
Minnesota Mining..........	17.4	14.8	13.4	14.4
McDonalds Corp...........	45.1	35.2	27.1	25.5
Merck....................	16.3	18.6	14.2	13.0
Monsanto.................	23.2	10.9	27.4	27.4
Northwest Airlines.........	33.1	29.4	36.3	25.1
Pennzoil..................	36.8	20.3	29.3	31.5
Polaroid..................	21.3	26.9	37.6	71.5
RCA.....................	22.1	16.7	40.7	32.5
Sears....................	16.4	10.3	22.3	14.2
Sperry Rand..............	26.6	26.0	22.9	22.1
Texas Instruments.........	21.7	23.7	30.2	25.1
Upjohn...................	24.0	29.2	28.2	31.8
Weyerhaeuser.............	20.3	15.0	30.0	20.7
Xerox....................	19.9	26.7	19.4	21.8

year. Where there are large changes in volatility, as in the case of Avon Products, Ford, or IT&T, either a major structural change has taken place in the company's fortunes or investors have come to view the company in a radically different manner. Polaroid, as a classic example, exhibited a stable 20- to 25-percent volatility as long as Wall Street believed in the magic of the Polaroid camera. When Eastman Kodak threatened Polaroid's exclusivity, a high P/E stock became a normal P/E stock, driving the volatility measure to an unsustainable 71.5 percent.

But, how does this relate to the price paid for an option, known as the premium? Perhaps the best explanation can be made with a picture. The graphs in Figures 3–1 to 3–5 portray the option premiums as they change during their life. There is a graph for five different levels of volatility, ranging from 10 percent through 50 percent. The scale on the left of each graph is the premium for the option expressed as a percent of the option's strike price. In other words, for our Atlantic Richfield July 100, an option premium of $1,000 (quoted as 10 in the newspaper) would be considered a 10-percent premium when compared with the strike price of 100. The scale along the bottom of the graph is the time remaining in the option's life, expressed in months. The curves plotted on the graph are the premium levels for a given ratio of underlying stock price to the strike price of the option. Again, for the Atlantic Richfield July 100, if the stock price remained at 100 the ratio of stock price to strike price (or exercise price) would

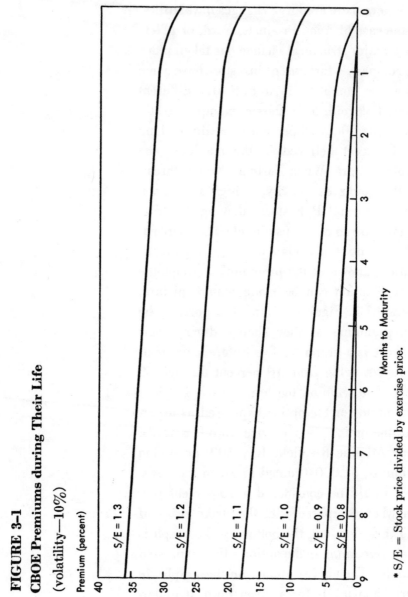

FIGURE 3-1
CBOE Premiums during Their Life
(volatility—10%)

Premium (percent)

S/E = 1.3

S/E = 1.2

S/E = 1.1

S/E = 1.0

S/E = 0.9

S/E = 0.8

Months to Maturity

* S/E = Stock price divided by exercise price.

FIGURE 3-2
CBOE Premiums during Their Life

(volatility—20%)

Premium (percent)

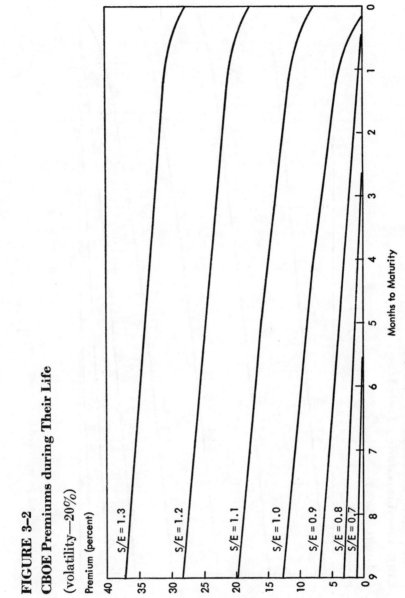

Months to Maturity

* S/E = Stock price divided by exercise price.

FIGURE 3-3
CBOE Premiums during Their Life

(volatility—30%)

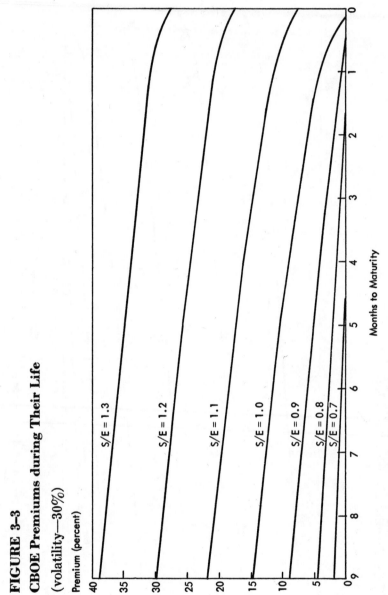

Premium (percent)

S/E = 1.3

S/E = 1.2

S/E = 1.1

S/E = 1.0

S/E = 0.9

S/E = 0.8
S/E = 0.7

Months to Maturity

* S/E = Stock price divided by exercise price.

FIGURE 3-4

CBOE Premiums during Their Life

(volatility—40%)

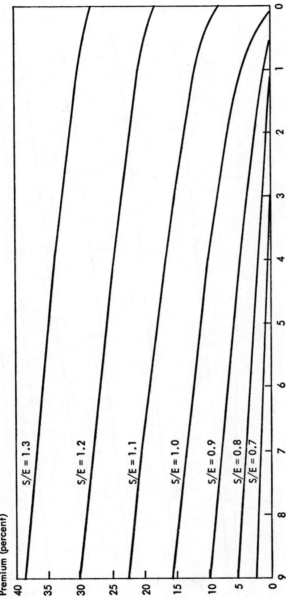

Premium (percent)

S/E = 1.3
S/E = 1.2
S/E = 1.1
S/E = 1.0
S/E = 0.9
S/E = 0.8
S/E = 0.7

Months to Maturity

* S/E = Stock price divided by exercise price.

FIGURE 3–5
CBOE Premiums during Their Life
(volatility—50%)

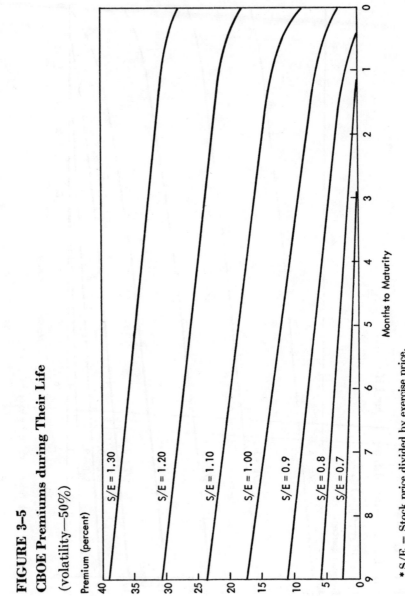

* S/E = Stock price divided by exercise price.

be 1, and the curve marked $S/E = 1.0$ would precisely describe the premium level during the life of the option. As Figure 3–1 of the "volatility—10%" graph, shows, such an option would have a premium of 10 percent at nine months; this would drop to 7.5 percent by six months, 5 percent by three months, then to zero slightly before the final day of trading. This curved decline occurs because the time value of the option is not purely linear and because the commission costs for a trader would discourage buying and exercising the option in its final days.[2] It is logical that the premium level is

---

[2] These curves were derived for the CBOE options by a least squares regression of actual option premiums sampled during a period when options were both over-valued and undervalued as measured by the Black-Scholes model published in the *Journal of Political Economy*, Vol. 81, No. 3, May/June 1973. In other words, these are empirical curves which measure a norm during a period when 90-day Treasury bills averaged 7 percent and for underlying stock with low yields.

For those investors who relate more easily to an algebraic formula, the following equations are presented as an easy method to compute premiums using nothing more than a hand calculator and the following table of the square root ($T^{\frac{1}{2}}$) of the time remaining in the option.

T	$T^{\frac{1}{2}}$	T	$T^{\frac{1}{2}}$	T	$T^{\frac{1}{2}}$
9.00	3.00	6.00	2.45	3.00	1.73
8.80	2.97	5.80	2.41	2.80	1.67
8.50	2.92	5.50	2.35	2.50	1.58
8.30	2.88	5.30	2.30	2.30	1.52
8.20	2.86	5.20	2.28	2.20	1.48
8.00	2.83	5.00	2.24	2.00	1.41
7.80	2.79	4.80	2.19	1.80	1.34
7.50	2.74	4.50	2.12	1.50	1.23
7.30	2.70	4.30	2.08	1.30	1.14
7.20	2.68	4.20	2.05	1.20	1.10
7.00	2.65	4.00	2.00	1.00	1.00
6.80	2.61	3.80	1.95	0.80	0.89
6.50	2.55	3.50	1.87	0.50	0.71
6.30	2.51	3.30	1.82	0.30	0.55
6.20	2.49	3.20	1.79	0.20	0.45

high for the longest maturity option, gradually tapering off as the time runs out, mainly considering that the premium compensates the option writer for the time he ties up his capital. The shorter the time period the less the required compensation.

The other curves in Figure 3–1, with denota-

Although the equations may look cumbersome, once the values of T, the time remaining in the option, and V, the volatility, have been determined for a particular week, the only change for each computation will be the Ps/Pe ratio. In fact, unless the call loan rate changes drastically from 11 percent and unless the yield is above 2 percent, the entire $(11 \text{-} Y \text{-} I)$ term can be dropped. With a little practice, premium estimates should be cranked out in a matter of seconds.

Option Pricing Equations

1. At or above strike price:

$$\% \text{ Premium} = 100 \cdot \left\{ \left(\frac{P_S}{P_E} - 1 \right) \left(1 - \frac{T}{45} \right) + T \left[.01 + \frac{V}{9,000} - \frac{(11 - Y - I)}{1,200} \right] \right\}$$

2. Below strike price:

$$\% \text{ Premium} = 100 \cdot \left\{ 0.4 \left(\frac{P_S}{P_E} - 1 \right) + T^{\frac{1}{2}} \left[.0267 + \frac{V}{1,500} - \frac{(11 - Y - I)}{400} \right] \right\}$$

Where:

P_S = Stock price

P_E = Strike price of option

T = Time remaining in option's life, expressed in months

V = % Volatility = $\frac{1}{2}$ $\left[\dfrac{\dfrac{52\text{-Week High} - 52\text{-Week Low}}{(52\text{-Week High} + 52\text{-Week Low})}}{2} \times 100 \right]$

Y = Annual yield on underlying stock

I = Call loan rate on money lent brokers by New York banks

$T^{\frac{1}{2}}$ = Square root of T

tions ranging from $S/E = 0.8$ to $S/E = 1.3$, portray the premium levels for options trading "out of the money," where the underlying stock price is below the option strike price, or "in the money," where the opposite is true. The equation $S/E = 0.8$ means that the stock price is 80 percent of the strike price and therefore "out of the money." An $S/E = 1.3$ describes an option in which the underlying stock price is 30 percent above the strike price ("in the money"). While this may seem a complicated diagram, it boils several of the key measuring variables down to a small family of curves, rather than a book of tables, and will be an important measuring device when we get down to the serious business of managing money.

The five graphs in Figures 3–1 to 3–5 reflect the higher premium levels caused by different degrees of volatility. Since volatility is a measure of the risk of owning a stock (the greater the degree of price fluctuation, the greater the risk of a severe price drop), the premium curves shift upward from one graph to the next in proportion to an increasing level of volatility. The way one reads the graphs is to first match the present volatility measure of the underlying stock for the past 52 weeks[3] with the graph having the closest level of volatility. Suppose that the latest volatility reading were 17 percent, then the 20 percent volatility graph would be appropriate. If we were to use our Atlantic Richfield July 100 option as an example, let

---

[3] As mentioned previously, the necessary data can be obtained from the *Media General Financial Weekly*.

us assume that the date is April 1 and Atlantic Richfield stock is trading at $110 a share. Dividing the stock price of $110 by the exercise price of $100 we would arrive at 1.1 as our S/E ratio. By means of the option calendar in Figure 2–1, we find that the first week in April is 4.0 months from the exercise date of the July option. Entering the premium diagram at four months, we move up to the S/E curve marked 1.1. Moving left from this point to the vertical axis we find the estimated premium to be 14.5 percent. To convert this into dollars and cents we simply multiply the 14.5 percent times the strike price of 100 and obtain $1,450 as the cash premium.

To make this task less burdensome for those who dislike multiplication and division, a set of graphs has been included in Figures 3–6 to 3–12 to convert stock and exercise prices first to percent premiums and then from percent premiums back to a dollar premium with the second set of graphs. This may sound like a lot of steps, but it is really quite simple. Remember, the key is the family of option premium curves for each level of volatility. To enter this curve you need the months to maturity from the option calendar in Figure 2–1 and the S/E ratio (stock price divided by exercise price) obtained from Figure 3–6 or 3–7. To obtain the S/E factor graphically, find the stock price on the left hand axis of the graph (in this case 110) and draw a line across to the right. Draw a second line up from the bottom axis at the point where strike price equals 100. Where these two lines intersect is the S/E factor. If we had not

FIGURE 3–6

Converting Stock Prices to S/E Factors

Stock Price

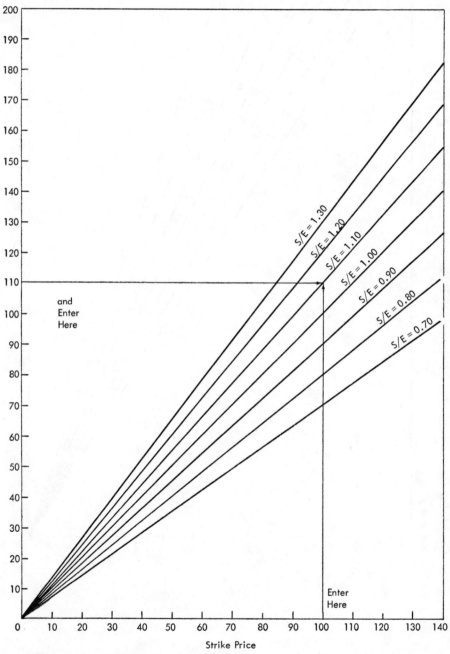

Strike Price

* S/E = Stock price divided by exercise price.

FIGURE 3-7

Graph for Converting Stock Prices to S/E Factors

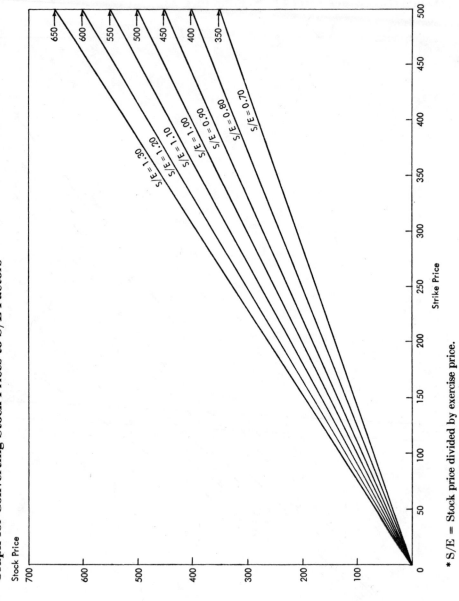

Stock Price

Strike Price

* S/E = Stock price divided by exercise price.

FIGURE 3-8
CBOE Premiums during Their Life
(volatility—20%)

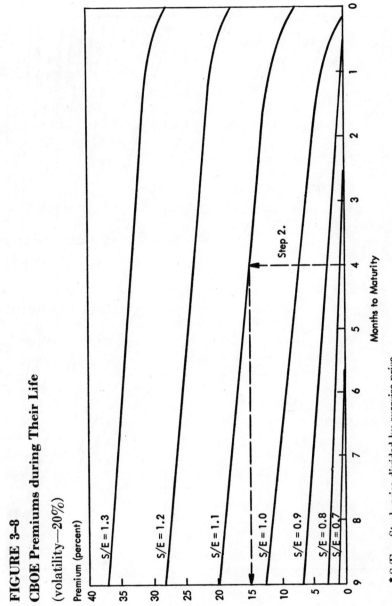

* S/E = Stock price divided by exercise price.

FIGURE 3-9

Graph for Converting Percent Premiums to Cash Premiums

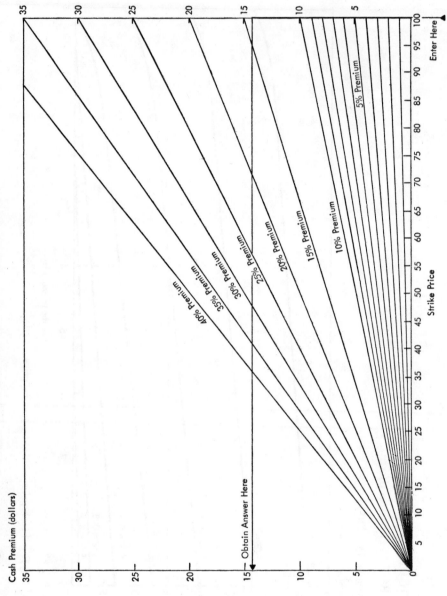

FIGURE 3-10
Graph for Converting Percent Premiums to Cash Premiums

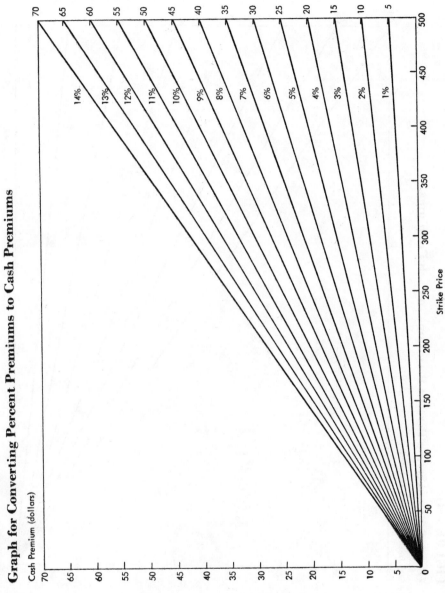

FIGURE 3-11
Graph for Converting Percent Premiums to Cash Premiums

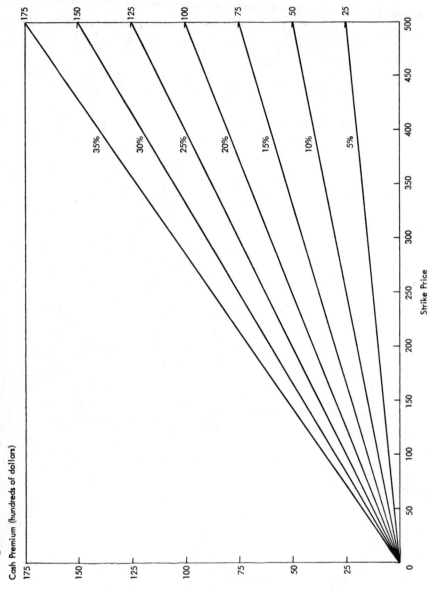

Cash Premium (hundreds of dollars)

175 — 150 — 125 — 100 — 75 — 50 — 25 —

35%   30%   25%   20%   15%   10%   5%

175 150 125 100 75 50 25

0   50 100 150 200 250 300 350 400 450 500

Strike Price

FIGURE 3–12
Graph for Converting Percent Premiums to Cash Premiums

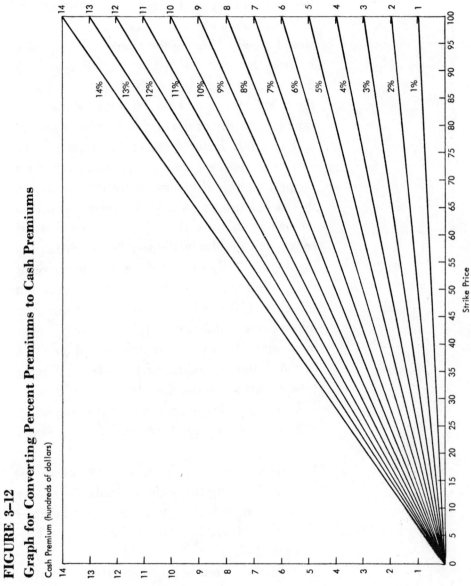

Cash Premium (hundreds of dollars)

Strike Price

used such nice round numbers and had arrived at a point somewhere between the S/E lines, we would simply estimate the number. If we ended halfway between the $S/E = 1.10$ line and the $S/E = 1.00$ line, we would obviously estimate the S/E factor to be 1.05. Now that we have the time to maturity of the option from the calendar and the S/E factor from our first set of conversion graphs, we enter the premium curve for 20 percent volatility just as we did before. In this case, however, we take the answer of a 14.5 percent premium and turn to our second set of conversion graphs in Figures 3–9 to 3–12. Using Figure 3–9, we simply enter the curve at the appropriate strike price on the bottom (in this case, 100) and move up to the proper premium curve (14.5 percent). The answer is read by moving directly left from the premium curve to the dollar premium on the left hand scale (see the arrow on the diagram).

In review, the procedure for estimating an option premium consists of the following steps:

1. Determining the time to maturity of an option by using the option calendar in Figure 2–1, and by calculating the S/E ratio using either Figure 3–6 (marked Step 1) or Figure 3–7.

2. Using the time to maturity and S/E ratio, enter the appropriate premium curve to estimate the normal percent premium.

3. Once the percent premium has been obtained, it is converted from percentage terms to dollars by using the final set of

conversion graphs, Figure 3–9, 3–10, 3–11, or 3–12.

All premiums calculated by the preceding method assume no appreciable dividend yield for the underlying stock. To be more accurate in the case of high-yielding stocks—i.e., 3 percent and over—the premiums from the estimating graphs can be corrected by subtracting the appropriate yield for the time period involved from the graphical estimation. The suggested calculation would be:

$$\frac{\text{Premium}}{\text{Adjustment}} = -\frac{\text{Time to Maturity}}{\text{12 Months}} \times \text{Annual Yield}$$

For a stock yielding 6 percent and an option with three months to maturity, the correction would be:

$$\frac{\text{Premium}}{\text{Adjustment}} = \frac{-3 \text{ Months}}{\text{12 Months}} \times 6\% = -\frac{1}{4} \times 6\% = -1.5\%$$

In actuality, option premiums tend to adjust downward by this amount when a stocks goes ex-dividend, so that dividends are an important consideration when estimating a premium. Your stockbroker should be contacted to determine whether an intended purchase or sale is about to miss a dividend payment.

The reader is now equipped to evaluate premiums and all this without one cent spent for computer time! The next logical step is applying these skills to the proper selection and operation of option strategies, which is the next subject.

Setting Strategies

4

Any option strategy applied rigidly for a long enough period will result in the loss of all capital. There is a correct strategy—or, in the case of the CBOE, there are several correct strategies—for a given market environment. The key is to define the environment and then match it with the appropriate strategies.

But, before getting involved in environments, what do we mean by a strategy? It is a set of procedures designed to attain a desired goal, which in this case is a profit on our invested capital. The process can be thought of in terms of a military campaign. We have reserves, our capital, and we desire to employ them to achieve a victory, a monetary profit. With great hopes and little experience, the initial instinct is to attack, to overwhelm the enemy with all our reserves. If we face a wise opponent, and the marketplace draws the most brilliant talent in the world, he lets us spend our reserves in one false move and our war is lost. Or, if we are more conservative, but unwise, we may fritter away our reserves in one false move after another.

As we grow older and wiser and gain the experience of our own losses and those of others, we learn to develop a second skill, defense. This learning sequence is true in all contests, whether military, athletic, or otherwise. The college star spends his first years as a professional learning that the key to winning consistently is to have a good defense as well as an offense. This is the only successful approach when you face stiff competition. The veteran who wants to play for many years avoids the one total burst of energy by which he risks everything for the sake of glory. It is glamorous, it may make headlines, but it is usually characteristic of a short, meteoric career. The pro provides a good defense to avoid being hurt badly, and launches a wise offense to capitalize on the weakness of his opponents. When he sees an opportunity for victory, he may strike firmly, but never in such a manner that if he is wrong he is destroyed. This concept is of utmost importance in our case, since the most significant feature of stock options is their capability of providing a stock market defense. Defense in this sense is the minimizing of capital losses as we go about our business of making capital profits.

As we mentioned in the introduction to the CBOE, its aftermarket for options permits the application of strategies ranging from a heavy dependence on market timing and stock selection, all the way to strategies which lack forecasts and assume random-walk stock price behavior. Investigating this spectrum is probably the best means of introducing the major strategies covered in this book.

The most aggressive option strategies attempt to use a minimum of money to gain a profit usually in excess of 100 percent a year for the money involved in the trade, if it works. Invariably, if the potential rewards are great so is the risk of loss. Most beginning investors are blind to this fact, not so much because they can't see that the risk of loss exists, but rather that they don't want to see. When personal money is involved, especially when it is a large part of one's bankroll, it is virtually impossible to be objective. The major enemy in the battle for profits is your own emotions and, when money is at stake, the most deep-seated and powerful ones come into play. It is amazing to see how many people engage in high risk/high reward strategies without ever considering the risk. At the height of a bull market, the spinster school teacher who hears about fortunes being made in the stock market takes her lifetime savings of $5,000 and doesn't buy General Motors, but 1,000 shares of an over-the-counter stock in a company with no business, with inexperienced management, with merely the promise of a new product that will change the world. She has purchased a dream, the chance to make a fortune, and instead loses it all. Or, the hard-nosed business executive, about to retire, who gambles his lifetime fortune of $200,000 on a new venture so that he can have some big money to retire on. Both of these people, who are by no means unusual, forgot or didn't consider their defense. A high risk/high reward strategy is fine, as long as the odds favor success and a small amount of total capital is employed. When little is at stake, you can take a big gamble with equanimity. When everything is at stake you choke up and lose it all. It's as simple as that.

The major strategies available will be presented according to their respective risk/reward class. This is done so that the reader can begin to match his goals and suitability with the strategies which are correct for him. Suitability should be a major concern for the individual in the sense that he should match his pocketbook to his investing. When using the riskiest strategies he should be able to lose all his capital without cramping his life-style or affecting his ability to pay his bills. Likewise, he should not risk all his investing capital in the high risk area, but rather restrict it to a small portion such as less than 20 percent. The safer strategies will allow him to risk more of his investing capital. As each risk/reward area is covered the strategies for both bull and bear markets will be presented, so that the reader will begin to see many of the reciprocal relationships which exist between puts and calls. To avoid confusion a table, Table 4–1, is presented which sorts out the various strategies according to the proper market conditions for their application. It might be helpful to refer back to that table as each strategy is discussed in order to see how it fits in with the other strategies as well as with the condition of the market.

The most common high risk/high reward strategies using options are the purchases of puts or calls, or the writing of uncovered op-

TABLE 4-1
Table of Strategies

Nature of Strategy	Name of Strategy	Risk	Reward	Ideal Price Environment	Profit Potential if Successful	Strategy Characteristics
1. High risk/ high reward	Call buying	Loss of premium	Limited only by degree of stock price rise	Bull market	100–300%/year	Requires the maximum skill in stock selection and market timing
2. High risk/ high reward	Put buying	Loss of premium	Limited by drop of stock price to zero	Bear market	100–300%/year	Requires the maximum skill in stock selection and market timing
3. High risk/ high reward	Writing calls, naked	Limited only by degree of stock price rise	Limited to call premium	Bear market	50–100%/year	Requires good skill in stock selection and timing
4. High risk/ high reward	Writing puts, naked	Limited by drop of stock price to zero	Limited to put premium	Bull market	50–100%/year	Requires good skill in stock selection and timing
5. Moderate risk/ moderate reward	Buying stock, buying a put for protection	Limited to the cost of the put option	Limited only by rise in stock price, less the cost of the put	Bull market	25%/year with no margin	Requires good skill in stock selection and timing plus premium evaluation
6. Moderate risk/ moderate reward	Shorting stock, buying a call for protection	Limited to the cost of the call option	Limited only by the drop in the stock price to zero, less the cost of the call	Bear market	25%/year	Requires good skill in stock selection and timing plus premium evaluation
7. Moderate risk/ moderate reward	Writing calls, fully hedged	Stock drops to zero less premiums collected	Call premium + stock appreciation to strike price	Bull market	15–25%/year with no margin	Requires good skill in stock selection and timing plus premium evaluation
8. Moderate risk/ moderate reward	Writing puts, fully hedged	Limited only by how much stock can appreciate during option's life less premiums	Put premium + stock drop to strike price	Bear market	15–25%/year	Requires good skill in stock selection and timing plus premium evaluation

TABLE 4-1 (*continued*)

	Nature of Strategy	Name of Strategy	Risk	Reward	Ideal Price Environment	Profit potential if Successful	Strategy Characteristics
9.	Minimal risk/ moderate reward	Writing calls, partially hedged	Stock prices move beyond breakeven levels	Limited by call premiums & stock appreciation to strike prices	Bull or bear market	15–25%/year	Requires good market monitoring, decision-making, and premium evaluation skill
10.	Minimal risk/ moderate reward	Writing puts, partially hedged	Stock prices move beyond breakeven levels	Limited by put premiums & stock drop to strike prices	Bear market	15–25%/year	Requires good market monitoring, decision-making, and premium evaluation skill
11.	Minimal to no risk/moderate reward	Spreading	Difference between premium income and cost of purchased option plus difference in strike prices	Limited by amount of premiums written plus long option appreciation to strike price of options written	Bull or bear market	15–25%/year	Requires good market monitoring, decision-making, and premium evaluation skill
12.	Minimal risk/ modest reward	Neutral hedge	Stock prices move beyond breakeven levels	Limited by call premiums + stock appreciation to strike prices	Bull or bear market	50% greater than the prime rate	Requires good market monitoring, decision-making, and premium evaluation skill

tions. A call is purchased to participate in an increase in price of the underlying stock. The advantages over buying the stock itself are that less money is required to purchase the option, while the option usually changes in value in proportion with the underlying stock. Therefore a small initial investment can yield a far larger percentage return than a simple stock purchase. For an OTC call the value of the call changes one for one with the underlying stock, but there is virtually no market to resell the call unless the change in stock price has been greater than the premium paid for the call. The same comparison can be made with a put option, only in this case the put buyer expects to profit from a drop in the underlying stock's price.

For the CBOE call options, the change in option value can be far from one to one with the stock price change if the option is well "out of the money" (as we shall see later) and only approaches a one to one price change if the option is well "in the money." This will hold true for CBOE put options when they are traded. The potential reward in all cases of buying options depends on the amount of price move that the underlying stock can experience during the life of the option. The option buyer is essentially purchasing a slice of time during which he expects a large stock price move to occur. Most option buyers don't understand this and rarely "cash in" their profit if a large price move occurs early in the option's life. The usual reasoning (call it greed) is that "if I made 200 percent on my money in one month, just think of how much I can make in six months." The investor fails to realize that such a price move occurs for one stock in a thousand, even in the best of bull markets. The risk side of the transaction is that the entire premium paid for the option can be lost. As long as a fraction of investing capital has been committed to such a venture, the investor can at least survive to play another day. The other high risk/high reward option strategy is uncovered writing. The tactic in this case is to write an option without owning the stock to guarantee the option in the case of a call, or without desiring to purchase the stock to honor a put. This strategy is essentially a gamble that the stock price in question will move in a forecast direction during the life of the option. In the case of writing uncovered calls the writer is speculating that the stock price will remain unchanged (if the strike price equals the current stock price)[1] or drop so that the call will be unexercised, allowing the writer to keep the premium he initially received when the call was written. In the case of writing puts, the writer speculates that the stock will remain unchanged (if the strike price equals the current stock price)[1] or rise so that the option will be unexercised and the premium retained by the writer. While the option buyer's risk is limited to the premium he paid and his reward is bounded only by the degree of change in the

---

[1] This may seem a minor technicality, but it is possible to write a CBOE option with a strike price below the current market price which requires that the stock price drops to or below the strike price to avoid an exercise. Writing a put is the converse.

underlying stock, the reverse is true for the naked writer. His reward is limited to the option premium, and yet his risk is only limited by the amount the stock can move against him, cushioned by the premium he collects. When writing puts his risk is that the stock price will drop from the strike price to zero less the premium he collects. When writing calls, the limit is how high the stock can rise above the strike price during the option's life, again cushioned by the premium income.

One might superficially conclude that buying options is far superior to writing naked because of the opposite risk/reward characteristics. This brings us back to the environment and the probabilities for success. In a bear market when most stocks are dropping in price, 80 percent to 90 percent of calls may go unexercised.[2] If an investor has a capacity for identifying stocks in trouble and times his call writing to coincide with rally peaks he can be extremely successful. And, with the CBOE, if he is wrong he can at least buy back his calls to close out his obligation and achieve an ordinary loss. Since writing puts is the opposite of writing calls, it makes sense that writing puts would not be an ideal bear market strategy. At the same token, buying puts can be an excellent alternative to shorting stocks in a bear market. There is more stress on timing and stock selection than in writing calls, but this is only because a stock has to drop to give a put buyer a profit. A CBOE call writer

---

[2] "Near-Total Wipe-Out," *Barron's*, August 5, 1974.

can make a profit if the stock remains unchanged, drops in price, or even moves up slightly, as long as the erosion in time value for the call overtakes the stock price gain. The major difference is that naked-call writing offers better odds of earning a good return in a bear market with good consistency, while buying puts can offer spectacular profits, such as 200 percent to 300 percent in a month when the buyer is correct, but it is unusual to produce such results consistently. The same can be said about the comparison between writing puts and buying calls in a bull market.

The next layer of strategies can be categorized as moderate risk, moderate reward. The benchmark is a pretax profit of 20 percent to 40 percent pretax on invested capital. The writing of calls fully hedged or the shorting of stock matched with the purchase of an equal number of puts would fall in this class. Writing calls fully hedged means that an investor buys or owns the same amount of a given underlying stock that he has written call options for. The hoped for result is that the stock will rise in price so that the call is exercised. The call writer then retains the call premium, any stock dividends declared during the period for CBOE calls, plus the difference between the purchase price of the stock and the price the stock was delivered at to honor the call. If the writer is wrong and the stock declines, the CBOE writer can either close out his position to avoid any further loss, or simply collect the call premium as a cushion against the loss in his stock. Since the emphasis is on making money on a rising stock price, this is clearly a bull market strategy.

The bear market analog to writing calls fully hedged is obviously writing puts and shorting stock on a one for one basis. The emphasis is on making profits by collecting the put premiums, while the short stock provides the guarantee for the option contract. Since writing a put places the writer in a position of having to purchase 100 shares of stock at the option's strike price if the stock declines, the writer stands to profit if the stock remains unchanged or drops. In this case he collects the premium received during the option's life. Since he guarantees to purchase 100 shares of stock at the strike price, if he has shorted the stock at the same level he ends up essentially covering his short when the put is exercised at the same price he went short. He incurs commission costs in the process, but otherwise breaks even on his short stock. If the stock rose in price instead, the writer could withstand a gain up to the amount of premiums he received without suffering a loss. Beyond that point he would face a loss of $100 for every point the underlying stock rose beyond the amount of the put premium. On the profit side, the writer is limited to making a maximum profit of the premium less any dividends on the underlying stock. An investor who simply shorted a stock that dropped sharply in price could make more money, but again the questions of consistency and defense arise. The covered put writer has both in his favor in a bear market, whereas the unprotected shorting of stock runs the frequent risk of encountering a short squeeze plus loss of sleep.

A variation of covered writing is the purchasing of options as a hedge against a damaging move either with a stock purchase or short sale of stock. The emphasis in this case is on making a profit on a change in the stock price either up or down, with the purchase of a call providing short sale protection against a short squeeze and a put purchase hedging the buyer of stock against a severe drop in the stock's price. In each case the potential profit is diminished by the cost of the option, but so is the loss.

The next layer of risk/reward, in this case minimal risk/moderate reward, involves a variation of the fully hedged writing strategy just discussed. The variation is termed the partial hedge and consists of writing more options than shares of stock purchased to guarantee a call, or shorted to guarantee a put. This strategy demands a separate chapter ("The Moderate Reward/Minimal Risk Strategies"), but the essentials will be covered here.

The main feature of the partial hedge is the establishment of adjustable breakeven levels above *and* below the current price of the stock involved. This contrasts with the fully hedged strategy which has fixed breakeven levels and where the protective emphasis is on the downside. The partial hedge's double-sided protection is provided on the downside, in the case of call writing, by the call premiums derived from writing. On the upside, the protection is provided by the fact that the gain in the price of

the underlying stock plus the premiums collected offset the loss incurred on having to purchase stock at the current market to guarantee
the uncovered calls of the partial hedge. The effectiveness of this strategy lies in the ability to
predetermine before establishing the position
exactly what breakeven levels seem appropriate
for a particular underlying stock. While this is
often based on experience, on the degree of
volatility inherent in a stock, and on measures
of past price ranges over time, some practition-
ers employ sophisticated probability models to
calculate the likelihood of a given breakeven
level's being penetrated. The existence of the
CBOE aftermarket makes this strategy especially
attractive because of the ability to adjust the
partial hedge during its life. If more upside
protection is desired, this can be provided by
reducing the net short position, either by purchasing more stock or by entering closing transactions for some of the calls. If greater downside
protection is desired, this can be provided by
writing more calls to generate more premiums
relative to the stock held, or some stock can be
sold in order to provide more premium protection per share of stock held.

While all the prior strategies mentioned are
most successful either in a bull or a bear market,
or are heavily dependent on the timing of purchases or sales, the partial hedge only requires
that too large an upward or downward bias in
the breakeven levels be avoided, especially at
market turning points. (Determining the proper
ratio of calls to stock is covered in the partial

hedge chapter, but an extreme stance would be 20 calls short and 100 shares of stock long.)

The most balanced hedging approach assumes an initial neutral position (with regard to changes in the market value of the hedge) which can easily be adjusted as the underlying stock price changes.

An important criterion for successful partial hedging when writing calls is that premiums are large enough to provide a good degree of downside protection without having to write too many calls relative to the stock owned. If this becomes a severe problem, the sister strategy, writing puts and shorting stock can be substituted. However, until the CBOE begins trading puts, a substitute strategy, which lacks a great deal of the same flexibility, can be employed, namely purchasing calls and shorting stock. In this case the inexpensive calls are purchased to capitalize on a hoped for rise in the underlying stock's price, while the shorted stock provides a hedge in case the stock doesn't rally and the calls drop in value or possibly lose their value altogether. This is really a poor substitute for the partial hedge because it depends heavily on a price forecast for success, while the partial hedge minimizes the need for a forecast and provides far more latitude in making a profit.

A much purer substitute for the partial hedge is a technique called spreading, which essentially substitutes the purchase of calls in the place of buying stock as in a partial hedge. Spreading consists of selling calls for a given strike price and expiration date, while simultaneously purchasing calls in the same underlying stock, but usually for a different strike price and possibly even a different expiration date. The usual procedure is to write two or three calls for a particular strike price and expiration date coupled with the purchase of a call for a lower strike price (usually near the current market price of the underlying stock) and the same expiration date. If this is done properly the premiums generated by the written calls more than offset the cost of the purchased call. In this manner if the stock drops in price the premiums from the written calls are kept, offsetting the loss in the purchased call, which has become worthless. With this approach the strategy has no downside risk. On the other hand, if the underlying stock price increases, the purchased call will increase in value, while the value of the written calls also increases. The maximum amount of money is made if, at expiration day, the underlying stock price is at the strike price of the written calls. At this point the premiums are kept and a profit has been made on the purchased call. If the stock had risen above the upper strike price level, a point would be reached at which the loss in the written calls would overcome the call premiums plus the profit on the purchased call. This is obviously the upper breakeven level. The attractiveness of this strategy is that less capital is required than for the partial hedge plus the fact that the spread can be established so that there is no downside risk. The one major problem is that a modest pocketbook may get in trouble if too many large price rises occur because margin requirements for the written calls increase as the stock price rises and the positions may have to be involuntarily unwound. The offset is that this trouble will occur in the vicinity of greatest profit so that the unwinding due to margin restrictions often proves to be a blessing in disguise. As with the partial hedge, the only price forecast required is that of a likely price range during the holding period of the options.

We are now at the other end of the spectrum, the random walk approach to making a profit with options. The strategy is termed the neutral hedge. This technique is basically an arbitrage between the degree of change in the value of the calls written and the price change in the stock purchased as the other side of the arbitrage. At a particular point in the option's life and for a particular strike price and underlying stock price there is a normative degree of change between the call premiums and the price of the underlying stock over a small range of several points. A particular set of conditions might produce a $\frac{1}{4}$ point rise in the option premiums for every point rise in the stock price. In this case a neutral position would be four calls short, 100 shares of stock long. For any minor changes around this level as much money will be lost on the short calls as is gained with the stock, as well as the reverse. If the stock moved to a higher price level, the ratio of call premium change to stock price change might be 1 to 2. In this case the position would be adjusted to approximate the new ratio, either by closing out two short calls or purchasing another 100 shares of stock.

How is money made with this process? In two ways, through the deflation of an inflated call premium, which occurs usually because of temporary market conditions, and through the loss of the time value of the call as time passes, both of which accrue to the call writer. The key requirements for success with this "know nothing" approach is an ability to evaluate whether a call premium is above a normative level and therefore will decline in value over time, and a monitoring system to flag such situations. In addition, an excellent trading capability is required to capitalize on these situations as they occur.

One caveat must be mentioned regarding the operation of any of the above mentioned arbitrage strategies. A United States taxpayer must always bear in mind that if a stock drops in price he may be faced with the unfavorable tax consequence of a capital loss, which is difficult to write off, and ordinary income, which can be taxed at a very high rate.

This broad brush coverage of a range of strategies should provide an overview of the most likely methods of managing money to be encountered if one uses options. It should serve as an introduction to the detailed treatment of the strategies which will follow and will include specific rules for establishing and closing positions, capital management, and the personal skill required to successfully engage in each of the strategies. Before going on, however, it might be helpful to review Table 4–1, which summarizes the characteristics of the various strategies.

It can easily be seen that the existence of a

bull or bear market determines the success or failure of many of the strategies, while timing and stock selection are a determinant of success for the high risk/high reward strategies. For these reasons, the next logical subject of investigation is price behavior.

Price Behavior

5

The paradox of Wall Street is that price, the determinant of stock market profits, is the least understood variable in investing. And while certain option strategies depend far less on an accurate price forecast than simply dealing in stocks alone, the need still exists to understand the price action of the underlying stock.

Price is said to be determined by fundamental, technical, and psychological factors, but most fundamentalists have a horrible record of forecasting future price directions, the typical Wall Street technicians have been disgraced by their lack of counter evidence to the random walk theorists who say that future stock prices can't be predicted, and no one seems to have organized market psychology into any measurable fashion. Where does that leave us?

Perhaps we can begin by asking how much money we can expect to make annually on the long side if we could forecast prices with any degree of accuracy. To accomplish this, let's review the behavior of the stock market for the past 25 years. Assuming we have perfect hindsight and can purchase a portfolio of blue chip stocks called the Dow-Jones Industrial Average at the lowest point each year and sell at the highest price later that year, what would our average annual gain be? The number is a surprisingly low 21.2 percent annually, considering how accurate we have to be to achieve that level. As Table 5–1 indicates, if it were not for three extraordinary years, 1954, 1958, and 1970, the overall average would have been 18.6 percent.

TABLE 5–1

25 Years of Market History: Picking the Exact Low and Best Succeeding High Each Year

	Low	High	Percent Change
1949	160.6	201	25.2
1950	192	237	23.4
1951	234	277	18.4
1952	256	293	14.5
1953	254.4	285	12.0
1954	279	408	46.2*
1955	384	491	27.9
1956	459	525	14.4
1957	453	523	15.5
1958	429	591	37.8*
1959	571	684	19.8
1960	596	663	11.2
1961	607	742	22.2
1962	525	659	25.5
1963	643	773	24.2
1964	755	898	18.9
1965	832	976	17.3
1966	735	828	12.7
1967	776	952	22.7
1968	817	994	21.7
1969	789	871	10.4
1970	627	849	35.4*
1971	826	958	16.0
1972	882	1042	18.1
1973	845	997	18.0
25 Year Average.			21.2

* Average is 18.6 percent without three top years.

Of course, these averages do not include dividends, which have averaged roughly 3.5 percent during this period. With dividends included the total return would be 24.7 percent per year for the full 25 years. At the other end of the spectrum, Professor Eugene Fama of the University of Chicago has estimated a 9 percent average total return by purchasing stocks in 1929 and holding them through 1965. Considering these two extremes, the potential profit of 20 to 25 percent for the safe partial hedge strategy discussed in Chapter 4 appears rather attractive. At least the profit potential of the more conservative option strategies should be placed in better perspective. The truth is that any equity money manager in the early 1970s would gladly accept even the 9 percent result.

What can we say about price behavior? Is it truly random as the random walk theorists propose? Or is there some order in the price madness? One phenomenon that seems to occur with a high degree of regularity is the major selling climax that has ended every major bear market for the past 25 years. (Some analysts have supposedly taken the cycle back much farther.) If one uses as a measure of selling climaxes the percent of New York Stock Exchange issues making a low in a given week the pattern is rather striking, as the graph in Figure 5–1 indicates. Except for several weeks in 1969, the minus 50 percent level has been exceeded only once every 50 months. As Table 5–3 indicates, a range of 45.7 to 54.3 months contains 90 percent of the variation about the 50-month cycle

FIGURE 5-1
The Regularity of Major Selling Climaxes

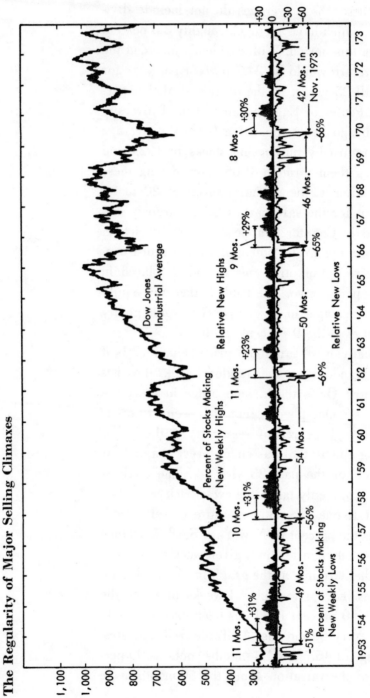

TABLE 5–2

Selling Climax Month	Time to Next Climax (months)	Time from Selling Climax to Peak New Highs
June, 1949..................	51	7 months to January, 1950
Sept. 1953..................	49	10 months to August, 1954
Oct. 1957..................	54	9 months to August, 1958
June, 1962..................	50	11 months to May, 1963
Aug. 1966..................	46	9 months to May, 1967
June, 1970..................		8 months to January, 1971

TABLE 5–3

Time between Climaxes

Mean..............................	50.0 months
Standard Deviation.................	2.6 months
Range.............................	46 to 54 months
90% Confidence Limits	
Mean − 1.65 Sigma =..............	45.7 months
Mean + 1.65 Sigma =..............	54.3 months

TABLE 5-4

Time from Climax to Peak New Highs

Mean.............................	9.0 months
Standard deviation.................	3.2 months
Range.............................	7 to 11 months
90% Confidence Limits	
Mean − 1.65 Sigma =..............	3.7 months
Mean + 1.65 Sigma =..............	14.3 months

mean. Perhaps even more amazing is the fact that, the majority of the time, the peak percent of new highs made in a bull market occurs from seven to 11 months after a selling climax low. This is probably the most striking example of regularity in stock prices.

What about the random walk theory? Is it valid or is it not? To answer such questions one should first define what we mean by a random walk. The term comes from a model of molecular behavior that describes something called brownian motion, or the fact that the molecules of a gas do not move in any well-defined path. The name random walk comes from the mathematics which describes such random molecular motion by assuming, as with a drunk, that a step in a particular direction offers no predictability of the direction of any future steps. The stock market analogy of the model tested whether a price movement on a given day had any relationship with the price movement at some fixed time in the future, whether one day later, 30 days or longer. The results of such studies[1] convincingly indicate that such a measure of price behavior does not show any link between the present and the future. This was a major contribution. The results convincingly proved that anyone who thought he saw a price pattern today which could predict with any degree of reliability a price pattern in the future was kidding himself. Experienced Wall Street money managers knew long before the random walkers that standard technical analysis yielded random results.

Where the random walk theorists seem to have gone awry is with the conclusions they have

---

[1] Paul H. Cootner, ed., *The Random Character of Stock Prices* (Cambridge, Mass.: MIT Press, 1967).

drawn from their research. The major one is that the stock market is a perfect market in the sense that all news developments are reflected instantaneously so that, again, there is no predictability in the news events. Such a conclusion not only lacks common sense, but leads to the ridiculous logic that, since the market is perfect, security analysis is a wasted effort. But without security analysts' processing the news inputs, the market would become imperfect, creating the need for security analysts because now there would be an imperfect market to take advantage of.

The common sense of the marketplace is that it is made up of people and there is a wide disparity between the abilities of these people to make money in the stock market. There is also wide discrepancies in the ability of market participants to perceive and understand the events that offer clues to future business conditions. And there is one correlation no scientist can deny, that of the long-run relationship between the level of profits and stock prices. All that the random walker can say is that a price wiggle today cannot predict a price wiggle either tomorrow or any other day. But that does not make the market.

There are a few successful stock market investors and they have one trait in common. They understand how the market crowd behaves and do the opposite. When the crowd has gotten excited about the future direction of stock prices and has moved them up, the professional sells. When the crowd is gripped with the fear that the world is coming to an end even though it isn't, the professional buys. He has learned by hard-earned experience that a price movement has stopped going up and all the money is spent when there is near universal agreement about how wonderful a situation is. A price can't go any higher unless there is a new buyer to enter the scene to pay up for the merchandise. If all passengers are on the train, the upward movement has to stop. The reverse is true when pessimism sets in. The price will drop until everyone who is disturbed by the fearsome developments has sold his stock. The price can go lower only as long as someone wants to sell some more stock. When all the scared sellers have sold, the price has to stop going down.

How can someone understand this process? No mathematician ever will, unless he leaves his equations behind and lives in the marketplace. The understanding comes from experiencing your own emotions as you attempt to make money in the stock market. By doing this and observing the emotions of others who are attempting to do the same thing you will find yourself wanting the comfort of buying into a well-established price move because you feel safe. At first you will buy at the end of every up move, because you have a lot of company. You have joined the train with the last passengers to get on board. When the price begins to drop you first become discouraged, then nauseated, and then vomit the stock, right at the point it stops going down. If you are determined to succeed you will keep trying, keep making mistakes, and then begin to realize why you have been wrong with almost 100 percent consistency. You *followed* the price behavior. Slowly you begin to see that you have to play outside of yourself. You have to let prices drop to the point that all the other price followers have sold. Then you buy. And when all the price followers have bought, you sell. You observe the other market participants around you who habitually buy at a top or sell at a bottom. Their behavior confirms your judgment. Any experienced broker can name at least ten of his customers who consistently buy at tops or sell at bottoms. People are the best measure of the market's position. Their nonrandomness would send a random walker back to his drawing board in a flash.

What is the answer? Does everyone have to leave his job and get involved full time in the market? Definitely not! The balance of this chapter will demonstrate some nonrandom price measuring tools that should offer some help to the part-time investor. Or, he will at least be able to realize his limitations.

In the chapter on setting strategies, Chapter 4, we mentioned the word environment. What we meant mainly was the price environment and, for want of a better term, used the terms bull market and bear market. In simplest terms a bull market is one in which the greatest percentage of stocks are experiencing a price progression of higher peaks and troughs with at least ten weeks between consecutive troughs or peaks. This is known as a stock with a major uptrend. If the successive peaks and troughs with a similar time period between them were moving to lower price levels, this would be a major downtrend stock and a market dominated by such stocks would be a Bear Market. Examples of both situations are presented in Figure 5–2. But what about a market dominated by neither uptrends nor downtrends? Logically it at least should have the possibility of existing. For the past ten years it has shown up for a period of several months, but quickly disappeared as the bull or bear market that had been in force prior to the period either resumed or changed to the opposite phase. It is important to be aware that such a market can exist because the short choppy price moves that dominate that kind of a market can wreak havoc on certain option strategies that are devastated by such short price swings (termed "whipsaws" in Wall Street parlance). Which leads to the question, how do we know what kind of a market we are in?

The commonsense way to define the current price environment seems to be simply to measure the composition of the market in terms of the percentage of stocks exhibiting strong uptrends as we define them, strong downtrends, or the residual of stocks going nowhere in particular. With a cut-off rate in appreciation or deterioration of 10 percent per annum, a ten-year study was conducted of the 100 largest market capitalization stocks on the New York Stock Exchange; the sample was broken into strong uptrend, strong downtrend or an "others" category on a monthly basis and the percent composition of each segment was computed. The graph in

FIGURE 5–2

A. Uptrend Stock

B. Downtrend Stock

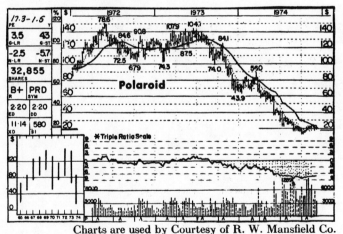

Charts are used by Courtesy of R. W. Mansfield Co.

Figure 5–3 is the result. Some very striking results become immediately apparent. Whenever more than 40 percent of the sample is exhibiting uptrend behavior, the Dow Jones Industrial Average plotted at the top of the graph is in an uptrend. And whenever the Dow Jones Industrial

FIGURE 5-3

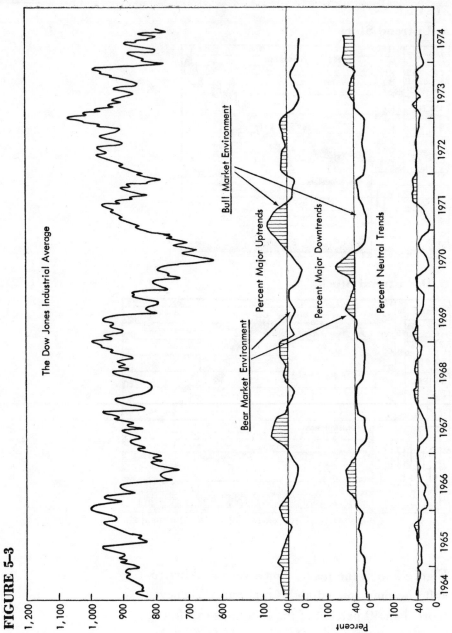

The Dow Jones Industrial Average

Bull Market Environment

Percent Major Uptrends

Percent Major Downtrends

Bear Market Environment

Percent Neutral Trends

Percent

Average is exhibiting downtrend behavior, the percent of stocks in significant downtrends is more than 40 percent. At key turning points, whether up or down, the residual measure is more than 40 percent of the total. So here, in very simple terms, we seem to have a tool for monitoring where we are. It doesn't say, "the bull market is headed for 1,000 in three months," but it tells us that, until proven otherwise, a bull market is in force and we should stress those strategies which favor such a market rather than attempt to accomplish something that the price environment does not favor. In addition, the quality of the bull market can be monitored in terms of the percent of uptrends because, in almost all cases, the peak level will be reached before the market top is made. This can warn of an impending change in direction or at least that it is becoming more difficult to make profits based on bull market strategies. Perhaps more importantly, the residual measure (percent neutral trends) can warn when price moves will be small and of short duration so that money is not committed to strategies depending on large price moves. For this reason perhaps the best title for this set of measures is "the market barometer, because it tells you the current price weather.

However, to make money in the stock market, more precise measures are needed than the market barometer. Through experience with the market's crowd psychology, several measures have been developed to deal with the swings in sentiment which so aptly describe price behavior. These techniques essentially measure something

FIGURE 5–4

The Intermediate Cycle Measure versus the Dow Jones Industrial Average

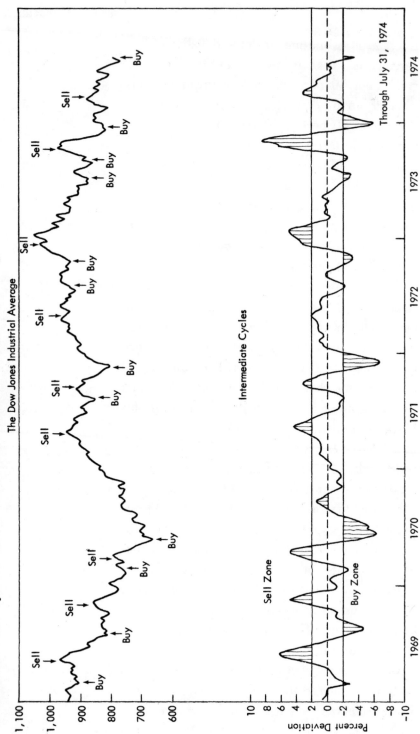

The Dow Jones Industrial Average

Intermediate Cycles

Through July 31, 1974

that the random walkers call "drift," or an extended price movement in a given direction. If measured properly, these "drifts" tend to possess limits which correspond to either overly bullish crowd sentiment or the reverse. A graph of the measure for 5- to 30-week price swings (the average is 14 weeks) is presented in Figure 5–4. To indicate the lack of randomness, the record of buy and sell signals for this method are presented in Table 5–5. The odds of just simply

TABLE 5–5

Intermediate Buy and Sell Signals for January 1, 1969, through July, 1974

	Date Signal Given	Buy	Sell	Points Profit (loss)	Percent Profit (loss)
1.	March 7, 1969	916.37			
2.	May 9, 1969		963.00	46.63	5.1
3.	August 1, 1969	824.23		138.77	14.4
4.	November 7, 1969		856.88	32.65	4.0
5.	February 20, 1970	766.54		90.34	10.5
6.	March 27, 1970		788.14	21.60	2.8
7.	May 22, 1970	665.66		122.48	15.5
8.	April 23, 1971		946.67	281.01	42.2
9.	August 13, 1971	890.11		56.56	6.0
10.	September 17, 1971		897.96	7.85	0.9
11.	November 12, 1971	817.24		80.72	9.0
12.	April 28, 1972		942.28	125.04	15.3
13.	July 28, 1972	937.24		5.04	0.5
14.	October 13, 1972	931.90			
15a	December 15, 1972		1,009.07	71.83*	7.7
15b	December 15, 1972		1,009.07	77.17†	7.6
16.	June 29, 1973	874.18		134.89	13.4
17.	September 7, 1973	888.40			
18a	October 5, 1973		956.80	82.62*	9.4
18b	October 5, 1973		956.80	68.40†	7.7
19.	December 14, 1973	?26.03		130.77	13.7
20.	March 29, 1974		852.32	26.29	3.2
21.	July 19, 1974	794.62		57.70	6.8

* From first buy.
† From second buy.

FIGURE 5–5

The Trading Cycles versus the Dow Jones Industrial Average

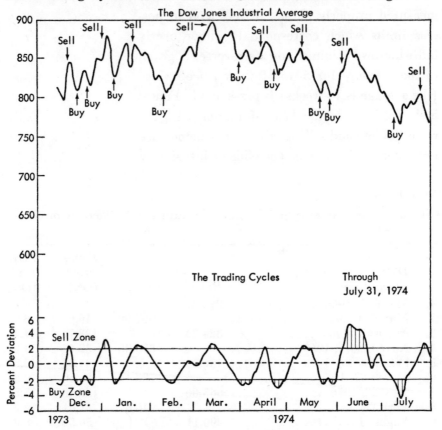

getting the price direction correct after each signal if this were a random process would be
0.0000002!

A similar technique has been developed for
catching shorter-term price swings in the range
of 5 to 20 trading days. A sample for the period
December 1, 1973, through July 31, 1974, is
presented in Figure 5–5. In this case a sequence
of 17 successful signals were given.[2]

---

[2] The timing cycles for the intermediate and trading
swings are generated by a measurement called an inverse

But so much for price swings. How about the fundamental and psychological influences which were the driving forces for the swings? This is such a complex subject that volumes of books would be required to analyze only some of the driving forces and behavioral patterns involved. However, the key to understanding the process is one word, profits. And it is not just the actual profit numbers themselves, but how our market crowd perceives the likely future level of profits. Many factors can shape this perception, but for the most part it is very similar to the race track; the vast majority of people depend on the touts. It is painful to be an individual. It takes endless hours of exhausting research to carefully arrive at your own conclusions.

Human nature and the natural law of accomplishing something with the least effort possible determine that most people are followers.

---

moving average. For the intermediate term a 30-week moving average of the Dow Jones Industrial Average is computed using the mean weekly price for each data point. The moving average is centered by plotting the most recent value 15 weeks behind the latest DJIA value. The inverse moving average is derived by then subtracting the centered moving average value from the 15-week-old DJIA point on the graph directly above or below and expressing this difference as a percent of the centered moving average. To bring the measurement up to date in order to characterize the most recent DJIA point, the centered moving average must be extrapolated forward by projecting a line through the most recent five centered moving average points, using this projection to obtain a current percent deviation. A similar technique is used for the trading cycle, except that a 30-day centered moving average is used along with the mean daily prices of the Dow Jones Industrial Average.

Those market students who wish to delve into such techniques in depth should obtain a copy of "The Profit Magic of Stock Transaction Timing" by J. M. Hurst, Englewood Cliffs, New Jersey: Prentice-Hall.

Who then are the opinion makers? They can be political leaders, the Chairman of the Federal Reserve, banking leaders, business leaders, the writers of investment advisory letters, the writers of Wall Street research or well-known money managers. All these people and more communicate their ideas and feelings to the market crowd through the news media, especially the *Wall Street Journal, Barron's National Business and Financial Weekly,* and the *Wall Street Transcript.*

Their efforts regarding an appraisal of the future level of corporate profits have to deal with the societal system within which a business operates. If money is going to be tight, businesses will be denied credit, so that they might get into trouble through the higher cost of credit, or they may even go bankrupt if they can't pay their bills. If the government begins restricting the freedom of businesses either overall or in a given industry the level of profits will usually be threatened. Therefore widely accepted fears that this will occur will depress affected stock prices.

Possibly the best means of understanding this process is to first learn in what kind of an environment a business prospers and then the environment in which business suffers. This can be based on personal experience or by observing what happens to different businesses under various sets of conditions. Then, the trick is to read the appropriate financial media to determine how all the opinion makers perceive the current environment. If you perceive a change taking place that the opinion makers haven't begun to talk about, and the stock price behavior supports your viewpoint, you are probably early in a particular price movement. If the idea warrants front page treatment, especially in the general news media such as the *New York Times,* the crowd is also aware of the development and you are most likely late in a price progression. This is the process, and unfortunately it is not easy to teach. The interested student will have to study and experience for himself for many years until he understands the process enough to function profitably. Fortunately there are option strategies which circumvent the need for such in-depth study, but they offer a modest return on investment. The greater rewards require harder work.

The foregoing comments are not meant to communicate a feeling of hopelessness, because fortunately the major psychological inputs can be organized and measured to a degree. The following analysis is an attempt to put such order in an otherwise confusing world of market developments.

A financial editor once made the statement that even Albert Einstein could never design an equation to describe stock price behavior because there would be a near infinite number of variables and the interrelationships would be too complex and ever-changing. He is probably correct but what about designing a weekly equation based on the major factors being considered by the market opinion makers? Table 5–6 presents just such an analysis for the week of July 21,

TABLE 5–6

The Psychological Equation

Variable	Current Direction	Price Effect
1. Credit system* instability	Negative	Negative
2. Interest rates*	Near-term trend up, but possibly turning	Positive. if interest rates do, in fact, turn down
3. Dow Jones Industrial Average	Positive near-term	Positive
4. Brokerage house profitability	Negative	Negative
5. Rate of inflation	Rate moderating from recent excessive levels	Positive
6. Presidential crisis	Negative	Negative
7. International oil prices	Beginning to drop	Positive
8. Middle East peace	Positive	Positive if progress on Syrian Israeli disengagement
9. Corporate profits	Increasing at a decreasing rate	Positive for positive earnings changes, negative if earnings change is negative
10. GNP growth	Growth rate negative	Negative as indication that economy is slowing
11. Foreign exchange rate of dollar	Somewhat stronger	Positive if dollar rises, negative if dollar falls

* Credit system instability and interest rates continue to dominate the investing scene. A true market recovery continues to depend on these two key variables.

1974. The important variables are ranked by order of importance from the most important, credit system instability, all the way down to the foreign exchange rate of the dollar. The ranking is determined by measuring both the frequency of occurrence of such items in the financial news media, and the impact on price changes in the marketplace as the news items are published in the *Dow Jones News Ticker*. The trend of the variables is listed for each variable, as well as the price effect. This is done to assist in determining whether the effect of the variable is likely to continue or whether a change in direction is taking place. The price effect is stressed because too often the effect is opposite to what most analysts might think. For example, at times the evidence of price inflation is a positive driving force when the opinion leaders are preaching buying stocks because they are a hedge against inflation. At another time the opinion leaders may be gripped with fear about government interference in business to control inflation and therefore the greater the inflation, the lower stock prices. This concept is especially important because too many analysts are tempted to analyze market behavior with fixed logic, such as "inflation is bullish," while the world around them is operating on a completely different basis.

This psychological equation, as it is called, can assist in price prediction by focusing attention on the most relevant factors in the marketplace. If interest rates and stability of the world banking system are paramount, the stock price detective should be best served by seeking clues as to important changes in these areas. The person who has the best insight in these matters should come out at the top of the competitive heap in terms of correct market judgments.

The true importance of the psychological

equation is that it helps explain the major shifts in sentiment which so characterize market behavior. Contrary to the believers in a perfect market, the major driving forces move in cycle-like behavior, first offering the appearance that all is well with the world, causing a market rally, then reversing or becoming less positive to end the advance or even trigger a rout. The announcement of the Arab oil embargo in October 1973 didn't drop the Dow Jones Industrial Average 200 points in one day; it caused a 200-point decline until the beginning of December as the true impact of the decision began to manifest itself. Yet, there were experienced money managers who understand the market's abhorrence of a major negative development of unknown proportions and who sold a great deal of stock in October to successfully avoid the "perfect market's" six-week slump. The part of such behavior that throws the random walkers off guard is that fact that these shifts in sentiment occur at randomly spaced intervals and exhibit a wide degree of price change between shifts. The trick is to recognize the cycle-like turn as it is occurring. The psychological equation will assist in recognizing this as will the monitoring of opinion maker sentiment. In October 1973, a great deal of money had been spent on a widely accepted thesis that there would be a worldwide shortage in many basis raw materials for years to come. There was near unanimity that prices were headed much higher, the perfect description of a cyclical top. And six weeks later, at the height of the oil embargo, there was near universal despair about the future of the Western World, thus a cyclical low. It is almost as simple as that the market needs good news to drive prices up and with no news or bad news prices will fall. And, if the psychology has reached one of its poles, the market will even invent an excuse to change direction. This is what Gerald Loeb means by "the market makes the news." How does one capitalize on these swings in sentiment to make money? While this depends on the strategy as well as the magnitude of the price move expected, the tactic is essentially to use the market swings as a guide to establishing or unwinding positions. The criteria for stock selection depend so much on the option strategy employed that this will be covered in detail for each of the strategies discussed in the chapters which follow.

But, to demonstrate the effectiveness of using the market swings, a study of the price movement of five CBOE stocks, selected in alphabetical order from every seventh stock listed in the *Wall Street Journal* quotes, is analyzed in Table 5–7 versus the intermediate buy signals of Table 5–5. Even without any regard for the existence of a bull market or a bear market, 81 of the 100 price moves occurred in the predicted direction, and the average gains exceeded the average losses in all cases. This should offer some credence to the methodology presented in this chapter, namely, the cross-checking of crowd behavior with price swings to determine whether the market is at a cycle-like turning point.

Fortunately the individual is not completely alone in his analysis of price movements. The

TABLE 5–7

The Effect of Market Buy and Sell Signals on Five Randomly Selected CBOE Stocks

Date/Signal		AT&T Price	AT&T Percent Profit (loss)	Exxon Price	Exxon Percent Profit (loss)	Int'l Harvester Price	Int'l Harvester Percent Profit (loss)	Monsanto Price	Monsanto Percent Profit (loss)	Texas Instruments Price	Texas Instruments Percent Profit (loss)
March 7, 1969,	Buy	51¾		79⅛		33⅞		47⅝		102¾	
May 9, 1969,	Sell	57¼	+10.6	84	+ 6.2	32½	− 4.1	48⅞	+ 2/6	123⅝	+20.3
Aug. 1, 1969,	Buy	52¼	+ 8.7	72¼	+14.0	29⅛	+10.4	45¼	+ 7.4	118¼	+ 4.3
Nov. 7, 1969,	Sell	53½	+ 2.4	65⅛	− 9.9	28	− 3.9	41	− 9.4	125¾	+ 6.3
Feb. 20, 1970,	Buy	50¼	+ 6.1	54⅞	+15.7	27½	+ 1.8	32⅛	+21.6	129¾	− 2.8
March 27, 1970,	Sell	52¾	+ 5.0	57¾	+ 5.2	28½	+ 3.6	34¾	+ 8.2	119	− 7.9
May 22, 1970,	Buy	43½	+17.5	51¼	+11.3	23¼	+22.6	29½	+15.1	83⅝	+29.7
April 23, 1971,	Sell	48⅝	+11.8	81	+58.0	28⅛	+21.0	44¾	+51.7	116	+38.7
Aug. 13, 1971,	Buy	44½	+ 8.5	70½	+13.0	28⅜	− 0.9	46	− 2.8	113	+ 2.6
Sept. 17, 1971,	Sell	42⅝	− 4.2	71⅜	+ 1.2	28⅛	− 0.9	50¼	+ 9.2	114	+ 0.9
Nov. 12, 1971,	Buy	42¼	+ 0.9	67⅞	+ 4.9	25	+11.1	44⅛	+12.2	104	+ 8.8
April 28, 1972,	Sell	42⅞	+ 1.5	69⅝	+ 2.6	30⅞	+23.5	54⅜	+23.2	149⅞	+44.1
July 28, 1972,	Buy	41¾	+ 2.6	75⅞	− 9.0	33	− 6.9	49¾	+ 8.5	171⅝	−14.5
Oct. 13, 1972,	Buy	47⅝		81¾		36		49⅛		164⅜	
Dec. 15, 1972,	Sell	51¾	+24.0	86⅛	+13.5	39¼	+18.9	50¾	+ 2.0	170¼	− 0.8
Dec. 15, 1972,	Sell	51¾	+ 8.7	86⅛	+ 5.4	39¼	+ 8.3	50¾	+ 3.3	170¼	+ 3.6
June 29, 1973,	Buy	50⅞	+ 1.7	98¼	−14.1	27¼	+30.6	51¼	− 1.0	83⅝*	+ 1.8
Sept. 7, 1973,	Buy	48⅞		87¼		32¾		60⅛		108⅝	
Oct. 5, 1973,	Sell	51⅜	+ 1.0	93⅝	− 4.7	35⅛	+28.9	75¼	+46.8	131¼	+57.0
Oct. 5, 1973,	Sell	51⅜	+ 8.6	93⅝	+ 7.3	35⅛	+ 7.3	75¼	+25.2	131¼	+20.8
Dec. 14, 1973,	Buy	48½	+ 5.6	90¾	+ 3.2	23½	+33.1	45½	+39.5	94⅝	+27.9
March 29, 1974,	Sell	49⅛	+ 1.3	80¾	−11.6	27⅝	+17.6	57⅛	+25.5	95⅛	+ 0.53
July 19, 1974,	Buy	43¾	+10.9	75¾	+ 5.6	23⅜	+15.4	63⅛	−10.5	87⅛	+ 8.4
No. of Profitable Transactions		19		15		15		16		16	
Average Profit		7.2%		11.1%		16.9%		18.9%		17.2%	
No. Of Loss Transactions		1		5		5		4		4	
Average Loss		4.2%		9.9%		3.3%		5.9%		6.5%	

* Split 2 for 1.

Value Line Investment Survey does an excellent job of presenting pertinent fundamental statistics for more than 1,500 leading companies, along with the most important company developments as reported by their staff of security analysts. *Investors Intelligence* offers a service which monitors the degree of bullishness or bearishness from a sample of leading advisory services, and Perry Wysong in his *Insiders/Specialist* report tracks the behavior of the New York Stock Exchange specialists who reflect in their behavior the swings in market sentiment discussed in this chapter. All of these services are advertised each week in *Barron's*.

If the eager student wants to become well versed in the art of understanding the stock market as detailed in this chapter he should read *The Wall Street Journal* daily and subscribe to *Business Week, Barron's, Fortune* magazine, and possibly *Forbes*. In this manner he will at least become conversant with the jargon of Wall Street and most of the major ideas that are driving prices back and forth in the marketplace.

The High Risk/High Reward Strategies

6

A ttempting success with these techniques is the climbing of Mount Everest among the various option strategies. While they are most tempting because of the large profit potential when an investor is correct, they are also the most demanding in terms of timing skills, the ability to make sound and rapid judgments and, most difficult of all, the discipline to properly manage your capital. As we mentioned in the chapter on setting strategies, the objective is not simply to make a profit but to operate defensively enough so that you can survive a string of mistakes and still have capital enough to make another trade.

While the market barometer can be a helpful guide in terms of deciding whether to use a bull market or a bear market strategy, some more specific timing tools will be required if one is to be successful. With this in mind the following techniques are presented as an aid. The techniques differ from most methods promoted by books on technical analysis which suggest taking action the moment an uptrend or downtrend line such as that drawn between points 1 and 2 in Figure 6–1 is penetrated. The alternate method

FIGURE 6–1

A. Detecting a Change in an Uptrend and Selling a Long Position

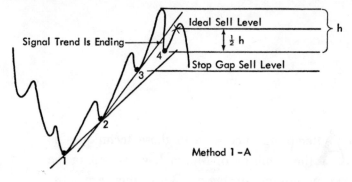

Method 1 – A

B. Detecting a Change in a Downtrend and Covering Short

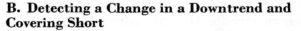
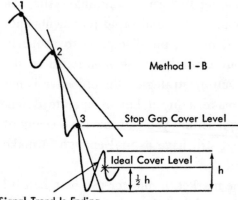

Method 1 – B

suggested here is to draw trendlines connecting successive troughs for uptend stocks and using the penetration of the most current of these trendlines only as a signal that a change is taking place. Roughly 70 percent of the time the price will not move past the point marked 3, but will reverse and resume its original direction. The

distance from highest point in the uptrend and
that reversal point 4 gives the measurement of
where to sell, one-half of the distance from the
highest price to point 4. The reverse is true for
the downtrend. In this manner the investor allows
the market to come to his price level. This is an
important advantage because the commonplace
approach of chasing a market that is running
away from you is avoided. And to protect yourself in case the price doesn't reverse, the previous
turning point 3 is used as a stopgap level to either sell or cover short. In this manner the investor is protected against all eventualities.

The technique for either buying or selling
short is a slight variation of the foregoing
method. (See Figure 6–2) In the case of buying
into a new uptrend, the same procedure is used
of drawing downtrend lines along successive
pairs of price peaks with the first penetration of
a downtrend line signaling that a change in direction may be taking place. Confirmation of the
change is a trough (5) which is higher than the
previous trough (4), the buy point being the first
point where the formation of trough (5) is de-
tected. In case this is a false signal, the position
should be resold if the price drops more than one
average trading day's range below the turning
point (5).

To sell short, the reverse of the foregoing
method is used. In this case the short point is the
first point that a peak (5) lower than the highest
peak in the trend (4) can be clearly recognized.
A short covering point should be established at

FIGURE 6–2

A. Buying into a New Uptrend

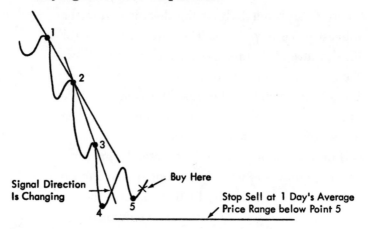

B. Selling Short into a New Downtrend

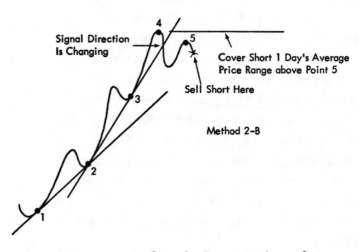

one average trading day's range above the turning point (5).

To avoid false signals several rules should be
followed. One is that penetration of a trendline
should be evidenced by an entire day's trading
range on the other side of the trendline from

where prices have been. Another is that an average daily trading range should be judged by inspection of a daily basis vertical line chart or better by computation of an average of the previous ten days' trading ranges. Once action has been taken either buying or selling short, the position should be maintained until a contrary signal for taking action occurs. In this manner if you are blessed with a large move in your favor, you should enjoy those large profits. The usual tendency of making an emotional judgment proves invariably to be wrong. The demanding prerequisite is to have the patience to allow these signals to occur, rather than anticipating what will occur and jumping the gun.

Several actual examples of the foregoing methods are presented in Figures 6–3 and 6–4 to demonstrate that the timing techniques do work for CBOE stocks. The important point to be remembered is that a predetermined measurement should be established to cover all eventualities. It is tempting to think that you will never be wrong, especially if you have enjoyed a string of successes, but you should be prepared at all times for a reversal. If you follow these general guidelines, you will be applying the well-worn Wall Street maxim of letting your profits run and cutting your losses short. What is usually left out is the method to accomplish those ends. With these procedures the option investor should be on sound footing.

Before going on to the rules for the specific strategies, a chart of the Dow Jones Industrial Average will be analyzed for the period of May

FIGURE 6-3

A. Example of Selling at the End of an Uptrend

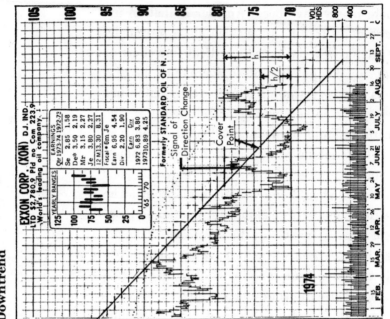

B. Example of Covering Short at the End of a Downtrend

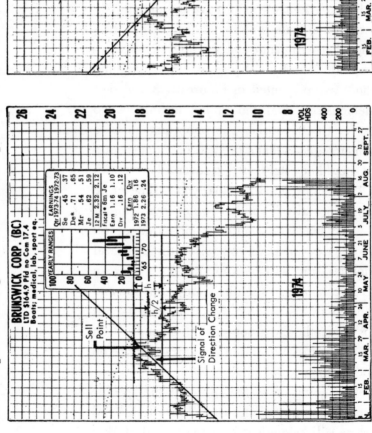

FIGURE 6-4

A. Example of Buying at the Beginning of a New Uptrend

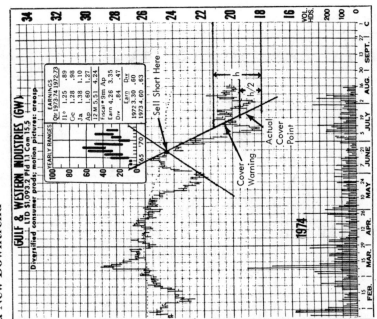

B. Example of Selling Short at the Beginning of a New Downtrend

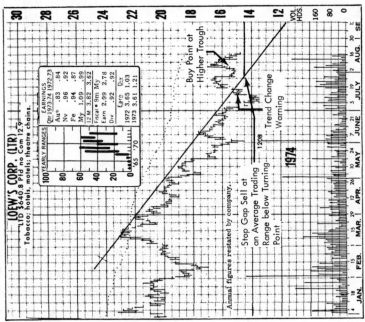

FIGURE 6–5

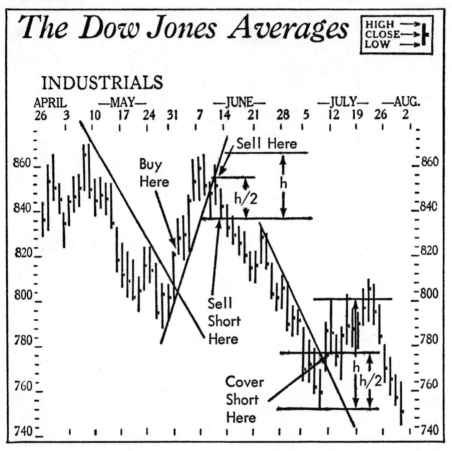

through July, 1974, just to demonstrate the general application of the price trend measuring techniques presented in this chapter. The graph used for Figure 6–5 was taken from the inside back page of the *Wall Street Journal*.

The first buy signal was given by the index's first penetrating a downtrend line, thus signaling the change in direction, and then rallying above the previous peak. This is the exception occurring, as the index failed to drop back to the $\frac{1}{2} h$ level. The sell signal which occurred next worked according to the odds and yielded a profit from the buy point. A sell short signal was given immediately thereafter. The cover short signal also worked according to the usual pattern, yielding a profit which capitalized on nearly 80 percent of the drop. Some traders may prefer to do this type of market average analysis as a cross check against their individual stock work, preferring to execute trades in sympathy with general market moves. This, in fact, is the recommended procedure.

The first strategies to be treated will be the high risk/high reward methods to be applied in a bull market. These are buying calls and selling puts naked. Referring back to the chapter on price behavior, a bull market is one in which stocks with strong major uptrends dominate the market. For this reason, the stock selected should exhibit uptrend behavior as defined by successively rising peaks and troughs with ten or more weeks between each peak. A weekly basis stock chart service such as R. W. Mansfield's, 2 Journal Square, Jersey City, New Jersey, is an ideal tool for such a screen. For buying calls the suggested procedure is as follows:

1. Buy calls only in a bull market as determined by the measurements of the market barometer.
2. Select those stocks with major uptrend behavior and with healthy fundamentals. Avoid a controversial situation.

3. The point to make a commitment is at the end of an intermediate length decline (5 to 20 weeks) as signalled by Perry Wysong's *Specialist Analysis* or a methodology similar to that presented in Chapter 5, which indicates that while crowd sentiment is extremely bearish after a decline, individual stock prices are beginning to improve.

4. Select your candidates from those exhibiting 20 percent or greater volatility as measured in Chapter 3.

5. Select four or five situations to diversify your position and protect against disappointment in a single commitment. The options should have a minimum of two to three months of life remaining and should have strike prices within 5 percent of the current price of the underlying stock.

6. Use buy signals such as those presented in this chapter for the underlying stock to time your purchase.

    a. when the signal is given, place buy orders for the options at the market price for the option plus a $\frac{1}{16}$ point discretion on options trading at 1 or less, $\frac{1}{8}$ point discretion for those above 1 up to 5, and a $\frac{1}{4}$ point discretion above 5. Have your broker put the orders on the board broker's book.

7. Ideally, the option premium should be no more than 25 percent above fair value as determined from the pricing graphs in Chapter 3. The preference is for options trading below fair value.

8. Commit no more than 40 percent of your trading capital to your entire position. This money should be thought of as maximum risk capital, which could be entirely lost without changing your life style one iota.

9. Each call commitment should be monitored daily by updating either a published set of stock charts, or your own for each underlying stock, so that the position can be closed out as each stock reaches first its warning point, then the actual sell point.

By following these rules, the option trader should have the odds in his favor of making profits with a good degree of consistency, while avoiding most of the pitfalls which rob traders not only of their profits but their hard earned capital as well.

The other high reward/high risk strategy for a bull market is the naked writing of puts. While this vehicle is not currently available on a National Securities Exchange, they should be traded by the end of 1975. It is recommended that the trader wait for such a development rather than writing OTC puts. The advantages of the after-market, so heavily stressed in Chapter 3, apply especially to puts, and the trader should deal only in a vehicle which offers him the greatest chance for success. However, rather than waiting until 1975, the general guidelines for writing puts naked will be outlined.

The objective of writing a put naked is to collect the put premium without ever having to honor the put contract. This contractual obligation requires the put seller (writer) to purchase 100 shares of the put's underlying stock at the strike price at any time during the life of the put. Quite naturally, as long as the underlying stock price remains at or above the strike price, there is no advantage for the put buyer to exercise his put. Logically, then, the put writer should want to write a put in the underlying stock of a well thought of, fundamentally healthy company, with a greater than fair value premium, at a time when the overall market and the underlying stock are beginning to rally. Since the put writer's obligation can be no more than the face value of the stock of the puts he writes, the writer should have a reserve, in case his timing judgment is wrong, of at least the collective face value of his put portfolio at their strike prices, less the put premiums he has received. A writer might argue that he can use margin in case he gets in trouble so that he doesn't need to completely cover all his put obligations, but this is highly dangerous. It is bad enough to lose your own capital, let alone some that you have borrowed. Once headed in this direction a string of mistakes is likely to occur and the losses on borrowed money could wipe out your capital. This comes back to the defense we stressed so heavily in Chapter 4. The overall goal should be to stay in the game, and not be taken out because of a few mistakes. Organizing this logic into a set of rules, we have:

1. Write puts only in a bull market as determined by the measurements of the market barometer.

2. Select as candidates puts whose underlying stocks are exhibiting major uptrend behavior, where the fundamental outlook is positive. Avoid a controversial situation.

3. The point to make the commitment is at the end of an intermediate length decline (5 to 20 weeks) as signalled by Perry Wysong's *Specialist Analysis* or a methodology similar to the one suggested in Chapter 5.

4. The time to maturity should be no more than two to three months.

5. The options written should have premiums at least 50 percent greater than fair value.

6. The put writing portfolio should be diversified to four or five different underlying stocks. The puts written should be trading with the underlying stock price at or above the strike price of the puts.

7. The writing commitment should be undertaken at the same time that a buy signal, such as described in this chapter, is given for the underlying stock. Place the orders at the market with $\frac{1}{16}$ point discretion for premiums of 1 or less, $\frac{1}{8}$ point discretion for premiums above 1 up to 5, and $\frac{1}{4}$ point discretion above 5. Have your broker place the orders on the board broker's book.

8. A fully invested position is one in which the capital plus premiums collected equals the total commitment to purchase the stock obligated to for the puts that were written.

9. Monitor the daily price action of the underlying stocks just as you would in the buy call

strategy, closing out the position if a sell signal is given for the underlying stock.

An additional measuring tool will be offered at this point as a means of aiding in the selection of the specific options for the various trading strategies. This tool is the graph comparing the relative degree of price change in an option (whether a call or a put) depending on the current relationship of the strike price and the price of the underlying stock. Presented in Figure 6–6, the diagram offers a means of determining the point movement in a particular option relative to its underlying stock by defining first the time to maturity of the option and the percent difference between the option's strike price and the price of the underlying stock. For example, a three-month option trading at 20 percent below its strike price (read along the vertical scale) would only move 20 percent of the point movement in the underlying stock (read along the horizontal scale). If the same option were trading at the strike price, the point movement would be 50 percent of that in the underlying stock. The importance of this diagram is to indicate that for trading moves, a call trading at 20 percent or more below the strike price would have to enjoy a 10 point move in the underlying stock to move 2 points.

Even if the price of the option (the premium) is extremely low, the odds of enjoying a good profit with an appreciable change in the underlying stock price may also be low. A safer bet would be an option trading above the strike price, where the price sensitivity of the option

FIGURE 6–6

Comparison of Option Price Change with Underlying Stock Price and Time to Maturity

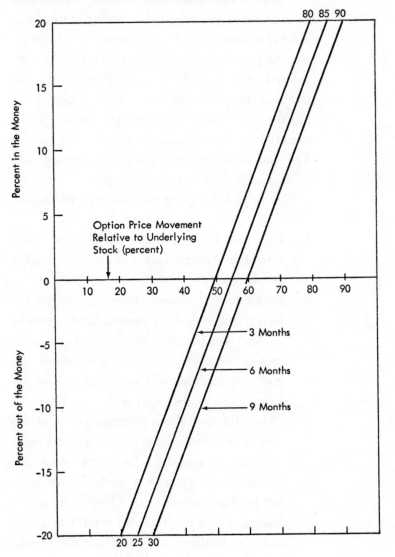

would be better than half of the point change in the underlying stock.

The next high risk/high reward strategies to be considered are those to be employed in a bear market as determined by the market barometer. Buying puts is the first such strategy to be considered and should be thought of as an alternative to selling short, the advantage of the put being the fact that if he is wrong, the put buyer merely loses the premium he paid for the option. The short seller incurs a risk that is limited only by how high a stock can rally.

The rules for buying puts are as follows:

1. Buy puts only in a bear market as determined by the measurement of the market barometer.
2. Select those stocks with major downtrend behavior and with deteriorating fundamentals. A controversial situation is a good choice, as many investors having doubts about the company's future will prefer to pull to the sidelines; i.e., they will sell.
3. The point to make a commitment is at the end of an intermediate length rally (5 to 20 weeks), as signalled by Perry Wysong's *Specialist Analysis* or a methodology similar to that presented in Chapter 5, which indicates that while crowd sentiment is extremely positive after on advance, individual stock prices are beginning to deteriorate.
4. Select your candidates from those exhibiting

20 percent or greater volatility as measured in Chapter 3.

5. Select four or five situations to diversify your position and protect against disappointment in a single commitment. The options should have a minimum of two to three months of life remaining and should have strike prices within 5 percent of the current price of the underlying stock.

6. Use sell signals such as presented in this chapter for the underlying stock to time your purchase.

    a. when the signal is given, place buy orders for the options at the market price for the option plus a $\frac{1}{16}$ point discretion on options trading at 1 or less, $\frac{1}{8}$ point discretion for those above 1 up to 5 and a $\frac{1}{4}$ point discretion above 5. Have your broker put the orders on the board broker's book.

7. Ideally, the option premium should be no more than 25 percent above fair value as determined from the pricing graphs in Chapter 3, using 80 percent of the call premium as an estimate of the fair-value put premium. The preference is for options trading below fair value.

8. Commit no more than 40 percent of your trading capital to your entire position. This money should be thought of as maximum risk capital, which could be entirely lost without changing your life style one iota.

9. Each put commitment should be monitored

daily, by updating either a published set of stock charts or your own, for each underlying stock so that the position can be closed out as each stock reaches first its warning point and then the actual short covering point.

The other high reward/high risk strategy for a bear market is the naked writing of calls. The objective is for the calls to expire unexercised so that the investor does not have to honor the call obligation if they are exercised. The defense in this case is the limiting of the position to the amount of money, including the call premiums received, to honor the calls if every one was exercised. If done correctly, this eventuality should rarely arise. However, the intelligent investor should be prepared for the worst. The rules for writing calls naked are as follows:

1. Write calls only in a bear market as determined by the measurements of the market barometer.
2. Select as candidates calls whose underlying stocks are exhibiting major downtrend behavior, in which the fundamental outlook is negative. A controversial situation is usually a good choice.
3. The point to make the commitment is at the end of an intermediate length rally (5 to 20 weeks) as signalled by Perry Wysong's *Specialist Analysis* or a methodology similar to the one suggested in Chapter 5.
4. The time to maturity should be no more than two to three months.

5. The options written should have premiums at least 50 percent greater than fair value as determined by the premium pricing curves of Chapter 3.

6. The call writing portfolio should be diversified to four or five different underlying stocks. The calls written should be trading with the underlying stock price at or below the strike price of the calls.

7. The writing commitment should be undertaken at the same time that a sell signal such as described in this chapter is given for the underlying stock. Place the order at the market with $\frac{1}{16}$ point discretion from premiums of 1 or less, $\frac{1}{8}$ point discretion for premiums above 1 up to 5, and $\frac{1}{4}$ point discretion above 5. Have your broker place the orders on the board brokers book.

8. A fully invested position is one in which the capital plus premiums collected equals the total commitment to purchase and deliver the stock obligated to for which the calls were written.

9. Monitor the daily price action of the underlying stocks just as you would in the buy put strategy, closing out the position if a short cover signal is given for the underlying stock.

In choosing one of these strategies, the investor should experiment with one or the other until he finds which one he is most comfortable with for a given market environment. He should then stick to that strategy, perfecting his skill until his capital has been built up to a substantial enough amount and he desires a safer, more defensive strategy, or until the price environment changes from bullish to bearish. This procedure is recommended because switching back and forth from one strategy to another will never allow the investor to become truly proficient at making money with a high degree of consistency. The investor may note that following the foregoing rules may require him to sit in cash during a bull market or a bear market, waiting for the ideal climate to establish a position. This is one of the great keys to success. It is the emotionally spurred search for constant action that causes the vast majority of losses. This is where the demands of patience and discipline are most crucial.

The Moderate Risk/ Moderate Reward Strategies

7

W hile requiring good timing and selection skills, the strategies covered in this chapter are far less high strung than those of Chapter 6. The two bull market strategies are:

1. Buying stock coupled with the purchase of a put for protection in case the stock declines.
2. Writing calls and purchasing an equivalent amount of stock, the goal being to collect the call premiums in order to augment the capital appreciation in the stock.

The two bear market strategies are:

1. Shorting stock while purchasing a call for protection in case the stock rallies.
2. Writing puts while shorting an equivalent amount of stock as a protected means of making money on the decline in a stock's price. The goal is to augment capital gains from the stock's decline by collecting put premiums.

Shorting stock, buying a call for protection and purchasing stock, buying a put for protection, emphasize the stock side of the transaction and are mainly a more defensive means of trading stocks than simply dealing in stocks alone. The mechanics of the procedure are probably best demonstrated with a few numerical examples.

Buying a Stock and Protecting the Stock by Purchasing a Put. Case 1

A. The stock advances substantially and the position is closed out.

February 1

	Debit	Credit
Purchase 100 shares XYZ Corp. @$50 a share................	$5,000	
Purchase a 6-month put in XYZ Corp. with a strike price of $50 for $500................	500	

April 1

The stock has risen to $60 a share and the investor decides to close out the position with a substantial profit.

	Debit	Credit
Resell 100 shares XYZ Corp. @ $60 a share................		$6,000

The investor decides to hold the put which is trading at $\frac{1}{16}$, as it may gain in value if the stock declines in price during the four months remaining in its life, or if the stock declines to a buy area near the put's strike price, the holder may wish to repeat the transaction. The result for the transaction is:

	Debit	Credit
Proceeds............................	$6,000	
Less cost of stock.................		$5,000
Less cost of put...................		500
Gross profit........................	$ 500	

$$\frac{\text{Gross profit}}{\text{Total capital outlay}} = \frac{\$\ 500}{\$5,500} \times 100$$

$$= 9.1\% \text{ return on capital in two months}$$

B. The stock is virtually unchanged during the six-month life of the put.

February 1

	Debit	Credit
Purchase 100 shares XYZ Corp. @ $50 a share...........	$5,000	
Purchase a 6-month put in XYZ Corp. with a strike price of $50 for $500.................		500

July 31

The stock price is unchanged and the option is worthless, since there is no advantage to exercising a put option at $50 a share if all that it allows a purchaser to do is buy stock selling at $50 and deliver it to the put writer for $50. The result for the transaction would be a cost of $500 for the put option which expired worthless. There would be no advantage in reselling the stock at the same price, so that the $500 put premium can be thought of as a cost of insuring the stock position for six months or

$$\frac{\text{Put cost}}{\text{Capital outlay}} = \frac{\$\ 500}{\$5,500} \times 100 = 9.1\%$$

reduction in capital during six months

C. The stock drops substantially and the holder of the 100 shares of XYZ decides to close out the position before it deteriorates further.

February 1

	Debit	Credit
Purchase 100 shares XYZ Corp. @ $50 a share...............	$5,000	
Purchase a 6-month put in XYZ Corp. with a strike price of $50 for $500...................	500	

The stock drops in price to $40 a share in two months and the put appreciates in value to $1,100. The investor decides that the situation will probably deteriorate further and therefore decides to close out his position.

April 1

	Debit	Credit
Resell 100 Shares of XYZ Corp. @ $40 a share...............		$4,000
Resell 1 put XYZ Corp. @ $1,100....................		1,100

The results of the total transactions are:

Proceeds from sale of stock........	$4,000
Proceeds from sale of put.........	1,100
Total proceeds..............	$5,100
Less cost of 100 shares XYZ @ 50........................	$5,000
Less cost of 1 put XYZ Corp......	500
	$5,500
Loss for transaction.............	($ 400)

$$\text{Loss on position} = \frac{\text{Loss}}{\text{Capital outlay}}$$

$$= \frac{\$\ 400}{\$5,500} \times 100 = -7.3\% \text{ in 2 months}$$

D. The stock falls gradually during the life

of the option until the expiration date, when the investor decides to exercise his put and deliver his stock to the option writer.

February 1

	Debit	Credit
Purchase 100 shares XYZ Corp. @ $50 a share...........	$5,000	
Purchase a 6-month put in XYZ Corp. with a strike price of $50 for $500...........	500	

The stock gradually drops to $40 a share during the six month life of the put, and the investor decides to exercise.

July 31

	Debit	Credit
Deliver 100 shares of XYZ to the put writer for a price of $50 a share (the strike price)......................		$5,000

The results of the transaction are:

Proceeds from sale of stock......		$5,000
Less cost of 100 shares XYZ @ 50.......................	5,000	
Less cost of 1 put XYZ Corp.....	500	$5,500
Loss for transaction.............		($ 500)

$$\text{Loss on position} = \frac{\text{Loss}}{\text{Capital outlay}}$$

$$= \frac{-\$500}{\$5,500} \times 100 = -9.1\% \text{ in 6 months}$$

The important concept to be understood for this strategy is that the largest loss an investor can sustain if the position aborts is the cost of the put premium plus any difference between the strike price of the put and the price of the stock when the position was established. Why this is so depends on the feature of the put option, which enables the holder of 100 shares of stock to deliver his stock to the put writer and receive the strike price of the put for his shares. The stock price could drop from 50 in our numerical example to a price of 5 during the life of the put, and the stock could still be delivered at $50 a share. If the stock had been purchased at $50, the only cost to the stock purchaser is the cost of the put and any commissions and fees involved in the trades. For someone who is probability conscious there is no better way to hedge a speculative purchase. And if the investor or his broker is alert, he may find very low cost options trading in the aftermarket which offer a far lower cost than the numerical example just given.

A set of rules which might be helpful for this strategy are as follows:

1. Since making a profit on a rise in a stock's price is the major emphasis of this strategy, it should only be applied in a bull market as defined by the market barometer.
2. The ideal time to establish such a position is at the termination of an intermediate decline as defined in the chapter on price behavior.
    a. For more precision, the timing techniques described in the last chapter should be helpful, both to establish the

position and to at least close out the stock side of the transaction.

3. Since the major cost of the strategy is the cost of the put being used for protection, the investor should seek call premiums trading at or below fair value as measured by the pricing curves in Chapter 3.

   a. It should be possible to find situations in which a stock is trading at $52 a share, and a three-month put is available with a $50 strike price trading at $200. The cost is the in-money value of the put at the time and is a good example of the inexpensive put protection that can be obtained.

The bear market strategy of selling stock short[1] and buying calls for protection is an extremely sensible way to trade stocks as opposed to shorting stocks alone. Again, several numerical examples might be the best means of demonstrating the technique.

A. The stock advances substantially and the position is closed out.

Shorting Stock and Protecting the Position by Purchasing a Call. Case 2

---

[1] Selling short is a technique for making a profit on a stock's price decline. This is managed by borrowing someone else's stock and selling that stock immediately for what is hoped to be a high price. Later, if the price has declined, the short seller enters the market, purchases the stock at a low price and delivers it back to the lender with all dividends received. In this manner, the borrower of the stock has enjoyed the fruits of a change in price, while the lender of the stock, who facillitated the entire transaction, enjoys the dividends as well as an interest fee for the stock he lent.

February 1

	Debit	Credit
Sell short 100 shares XYZ Corp. @ $50 a share..........		$5,000
Purchase a 6 month call in XYZ Corp. with a strike price of $50 for $500..........	$ 500	

April 1

The stock has risen to $60 a share and the investor decides he had better close out the position and absorb a loss.

	Debit	Credit
Purchase 100 shares XYZ Corp. @ $60 a share covering short................	$6,000	
Resell 1 call XYZ Corp. @ $1,100....................		$1,100

The overall result for the transaction is:

Proceeds from stock sale.........	$5,000
Proceeds from sale of call........	1,100
Total proceeds.............	$6,100
Less cost of stock when repurchased..................	$6,000
Less cost of call................	500
Total cost.................	$6,500
Loss.....................	($ 400)

The return on capital for the transaction is:

$$\frac{\text{Gross Loss}}{\text{Capital outlay}} = \frac{(\$400)}{\$5,500} \times 100$$
$$= 7.3\% \text{ loss of capital in 2 months.}$$

B.   The stock advances during the life of the call and the investor decides to exercise his call option at the expiration date.

February 1

	Debit	Credit
Sell short 100 shares XYZ Corp. @ $50 a share..........		$5,000
Purchase a 6 months call in XYZ Corp. with a strike price of $50 for $500..........	$500	

July 31

The stock has gradually risen to $60 a share during the six-month life of the call and the investor decides to exercise the call by taking delivery of the 100 shares of XYZ Corp. at $50 and re-delivering to the person he borrowed the stock from.

	Debit	Credit
Exercise 1 call XYZ Corp. and take delivery of 100 shares of XYZ Corp. @ $50 a share...............	$5,000	

The overall result from the transaction is:

Proceeds from short sale........		$5,000
Less cost of 1 call XYZ Corp.....	500	
Less cost of stock purchased on exercise....................	5,000	5,500
Loss on transaction.........		($ 500)

The return on capital for the transaction is:

$$\frac{\text{Gross Loss}}{\text{Capital outlay}} = \frac{-\$500}{\$5,500} \times 100$$
$$= 9.1\% \text{ loss on capital in 6 months.}$$

C.   The stock is virtually unchanged during the six-month life of the call.

February 1

	Debit	Credit
Sell short 100 shares XYZ Corp. @ $50 a share...........		$5,000
Purchase 1 call in XYZ Corp. with a strike price of $50 for $500.....................	$500	

July 31

The stock price is unchanged and the option is worthless, as there is no advantage in exercising at the same price as the strike price. The result is similar to the short stock-buy call strategy in that the call premium is the cost incurred for having a protected stock position for six months. The capital cost would be as follows:

$$\frac{\text{Call cost}}{\text{Capital outlay}} = \frac{\$500}{\$5,500} \times 100 = 9.1\%$$
reduction in capital during 6 months

D. The stock drops substantially and the holder of the 100 shares of XYZ decides to take his profit.

February 1

	Debit	Credit
Sell short 100 shares XYZ Corp. @ $50 a share...........		$5,000
Purchase 1 call in XYZ Corp. with a strike price of $50 for $500.....................	$500	

The stock drops in price to $40 a share in two months and the investor decides to take his profit. The call at this time is trading for $\frac{1}{16}$ ($6.25), but still has four months until expiration. Therefore, rather than selling the call, the investor decides to hold it in the event that the stock rallies and becomes an attractive short, the call once again providing him protection for his short position.

April 1

	Debit	Credit
Purchase 100 shares XYZ Corp. @ $40 a share, covering short.................	$4,000	

The overall result for the position is:

Proceeds........................		$5,000
Less cost of buying stock.........	$4,000	
Less cost of call.................	500	
Gross profit.................		$ 500

$$\text{Return on profit} = \frac{\text{Gross profit}}{\text{Capital outlay}} = \frac{\$500}{\$5,500}$$
$\times 100 = 9.1\%$ gain in capital in 2 months.

The important concept to be remembered for this strategy is that the cost of the call, along with any commissions involved, is the full extent of the loss that the investor can incur. For any investors who have ever attempted shorting this should be a comforting realization. Since the potential loss for the short stock is limited only by the extent that the stock can rise in price, selling short can be a harrowing experience, especially so with the bear market rallies as sharp and dramatic as they are. If one considers the general fear of rallies which short traders have, it is easy to understand why there is such a mad scramble to cover short positions at the slightest hint of a rally. If one uses the technique of buying a call when establishing a short position, it is possible to be cool-headed as one waits for the position to work. If the recommended procedure of shorting into the last stages of a bear market rally is followed, once it becomes clear that the market and your stock have resumed their decline, the call can even be resold at a small loss, while the short stock is allowed to enjoy the balance of its decline.

A suggested set of rules for this strategy follows:

1. Since the major objective of this strategy is to make profits by declines in stock prices, it should be applied only in a bear market as defined by the market barometer.
2. The ideal time to establish such a position is at the termination of an intermediate advance as defined in the chapter on price behavior.
    a. for more precision, the timing techniques described in the last chapter should be helpful, both in establishing the short position and especially in closing out the position on weakness rather than getting caught up in a short squeeze, as all too frequently happens.
3. The investor should seek to purchase calls which are trading at or below fair value as measured by the pricing curves presented in Chapter 3. The investor should also be on the lookout for special pricing situations, such as mentioned for buying puts, in which

the investor may be able to pay no more
than the in-money value of the option.

Fully hedged call writing is probably the most
widely known and most popular option strategy.
It has been used for centuries by a small number
of sophisticated investors who establish themselves as the bankers for the buyers of call options. Whether by writing calls against low-
priced stock owned in an estate or by purchasing
stock in order to write calls, these investors have
reputedly been able to earn 15 to 25 percent pretax on their capital when averaged out over five
or more years. The strategy's emphasis is to earn
the premiums on the calls the writer guarantees.
The stock which is purchased is thought of as a
capital investment in the option writing business,
just as a manufacturer would think of his steel
plant as a means for producing steel for sale.
Writing fully hedged means that one call for
100 shares is written for each 100 shares of
stock owned by the writer. And while it might be
tempting to be able to employ this strategy under all market conditions, the fact is that a Bear
Market will cause serious erosion in the project's
capital, in the form of the stock that is owned,
which is difficult, if not impossible, to match
through the call premiums that are collected due
to falling prices. The best environment to operate
this strategy is the Bull Market dominated by
rising stock prices. This is especially so with
listed call options, because the investor has the
best of all worlds. If his stock gains in price and

the call premium has appreciated to the point he would sustain a loss on his calls, he would enjoy a capital gain on the stock side of the transaction, long- or short-term depending on the holding period of the stock and an ordinary loss[2] on the repurchase of the calls. This ordinary loss can be offset against salary, dividend, or any other ordinary income received by the investor, who, by successfully employing this strategy in a bull market, can foreseeably pay all his taxes at a long-term capital gains rate and pay no regular income tax.

There are four possible conclusions for a fully hedged call writing position, and rather than omitting commission costs as in past examples, the following cases will not only deal in actual transactions on the CBOE, but indicate all commissions and dividends involved in the possible outcomes.

A. Stock Is Up—
Call Exercised

Date	Action	Debit	Credit
June 1	Buy 1,000 BS* @ 29¼ plus commissions....	$29,613	
June 1	Sell 10 calls BS @ 30 exp. 1/31/74 for $400		
	each..................................		$ 4,000
	Less commissions.........................		(118)
Aug. 2	Receive dividend .40......................		$ 400
Oct. 31	Receive dividend .40......................		$ 400
Jan. 31	BS is over 30 and the calls are exercised:		
	Sell 1,000 BS @ 30 a/c call...............		$30,000
	Less commissions.........................		(370)

* BS is the symbol for Bethlehem Steel.

---

[2] This is based on an April 1974 IRS ruling given to the CBOE which provides that closing transactions for calls previously sold should receive ordinary treatment, whether a gain or a loss.

Return on Investment

Proceeds..........................	$29,630	($30,000 − $370)
Plus premium.....................	3,882	(4,000 − 118)
	$33,512	
Less cost.........................	29,613	
Capital gain......................	$ 3,899	
Plus dividend income.............	800	
	$ 4,699	

$$\text{ROI} = \frac{\text{Total pretax profit}}{\text{Investment}}$$

$$= \frac{\$4,699}{\$29,613 - \$3,882} = 18.2\% \text{ for 8 mos.}$$

B. Stock Down— Calls Expire

If BS is less than 30 the option will not be exercised. Any loss incurred owing to the sale of the stock will be determined by the difference between $29\frac{1}{4}$ plus commissions and the selling price of the stock less commissions. However, this loss would be mitigated by premiums and dividends received.

For example, if we sold our stock at 25 our loss would be calculated as follows:

Sales of 1,000 BS @ 25........		$25,000
Less commissions.............		(336)
Proceeds.....................		$24,664
Cost 1,000 BS @29¼.........	$29,250	
Plus commissions.............	363	
Capital loss*.................		($ 4,949)

* The capital loss of $4,949 will be either short-term or long-term depending on the holding period.

This capital loss of $4,949 would be offset by the $3,882 ($4,000 − $118) net premium received which would be viewed by the Internal Revenue Service as ordinary income plus the $800 dividend income received for a total of $4,682, thereby giving a pretax loss of $267.

Naturally, each additional decline of one point in the stock would increase our loss by $1,000.

C. Stock Up—
Unwind Position

Date	Action	Debit	Credit
June 1	Buy 1,000 BS @ 29¼ plus commissions........	$29,613	
June 1	Sell 10 calls BS @ 30 exp. 1/31/74 for $400		
	each.....................................		$4,000
	Less commissions............................		(118)

Let us assume that on July 31 we received a negative research report on BS (then trading at 32) and we wanted to sell our long stock and eliminate our call obligations:

We would sell 1,000
      BS @ 32................. $32,000
Less commissions............ $ (380)
"Buy in" 10 calls BS
@ 30 exp. 1/31/74 for
      $450 each*................. $ 4,500
Plus commissions............   123

     * This is an estimated price.

Return on Investment Calculation

Proceeds from sale of stock @ 32...	$31,620	($32,000 − $380)
No dividends in this period........	—	
Original premiums received........	3,882	
	$35.502	
Cost of stock @ 29¼	$29,250	
Plus commissions.................	363	
Plus cost of "buy in" of calls.......	4,500	
Plus commissions.................	123	$34,236
Pretax Profit....................		$ 1,266

$$\text{ROI} = \frac{\text{Total pretax profit}}{\text{Investment}}$$

$$= \frac{\$1,266}{\$29,613 - \$3,882} = 4.9\% \text{ for 60 days}$$

D. Stock Down—
Unwind Position

Date	Action	Debit	Credit
June 1	Buy 1,000 BS @ 29¼ plus commissions........	$29,613	
June 1	Sell 10 Calls BS @ 30 exp. 1/31/74 for $400		
	each.....................................		$4,000
	Less commissions............................		(118)

Let us assume that on July 31 we received a negative research report on BS (then trading at 28) and we wanted to sell our long stock and eliminate our call obligations:

We would sell 1,000 BS
@ 28...................... $28,000
Less commissions.............. 357
"Buy in" calls @ 30
exp. 1/31/74 for $250
each*..................... $ 2,500
Plus commissions.............. 105

 * This is an estimated price.

Return on Investment Calculation

Proceeds from sale of stock @ 28..		$27,643	($28,000 − $357)
No dividends in this period.......		—	
Original premiums received.......		3,882	
		$31,525	
Cost of stock @ 29¼............	$29,250		
Plus commissions................	363		
Plus cost of "buy in" of calls.....	2,500		
Pretax loss....................	105	$32,218	
		($ 693)	

The important feature to be remembered about writing calls fully hedged is that the call premium affords downside protection for the stock owned, for the reason that the premium will be kept by the call writer if the stock re mains at or below the strike price at the expiration date.

The reader, after studying the foregoing examples, may react by saying to himself "why should I ever write calls fully hedged in a bull market? Why, I can easily pick a stock that will appreciate more than 18.2 percent in eight months!" This is a very common reaction, but

FIGURE 7–1

Profit Comparison between Buying 100 Shares of Stock versus Buying the Stock and Writing a Call with a $500 Premium

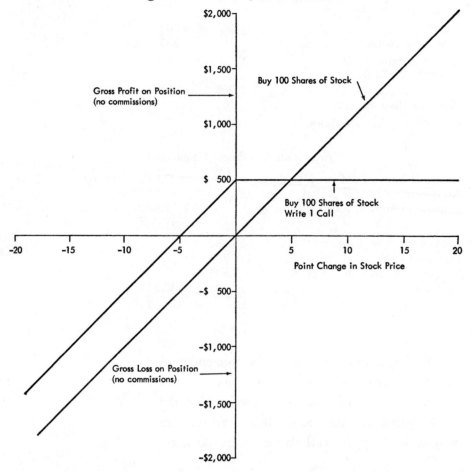

the laws of probability don't seem to back the statement. The diagram on the prior page (Figure 7–1) seems at first to support the idea that the buy stock strategy is the superior one. Above a five-point gain in price the buy stock strategy far outdistances the buy stock—sell call strategy. The key question is what prices are likely for the stock during the holding period? If a proba-

FIGURE 7–2

Superimposing a Likely Distribution of Prices over the Profit Comparison between Buying 100 Shares of Stock versus Buying the Stock and Writing a Call with a $500 Premium

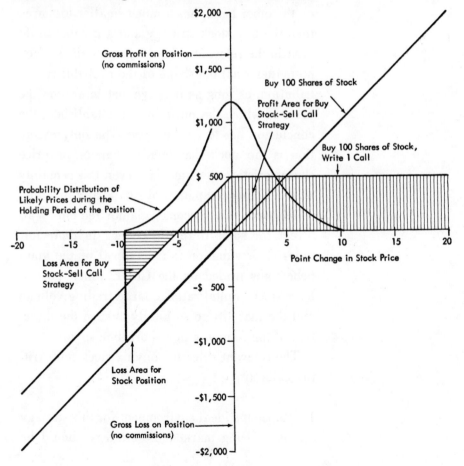

bility distribution based on a relevant history of a given stock's price behavior is superimposed on the diagram in Figure 7–1 an interesting comparison can be made. If the odds of achieving various price levels are used to estimate the overall profitability of the two strategies (see Figure 7–2), the buy stock, sell call will *always* have to outperform the buy stock strategy given enough trials over time. The reason this is so is that the buy stock strategy loses as much as it gains for every point on either side of the break-even level. The buy stock—sell call strategy, on the other hand, has a much smaller loss area than the buy stock strategy and a greater profit area in the relevant price range as well. In fact, no matter what the shape of the probability distribution, as long as it is symmetric around the price at which the position was established, the conclusion has to be the same. The only exception is the stock that totally changes its price characteristics over time. However, this is mainly true of young companies of small capitalization, which suddenly become glamorized in Wall Street for some dramatic change in their fortunes. This situation is not typical of the giant behemoths traded on the CBOE which possess huge stock capitalizations, large trading volume and the inability to so totally change the direction of the company in a short time span.

The relevant rules for buying stock and writing calls are:

1. Since the ideal environment for this strategy is a rising market, the strategy should be

implemented in a Bull Market as defined by the market barometer.

2. The ideal time to establish such a position depends greatly on the objective the investor is attempting to achieve. If he desires a capital gain on his stock coupled with an ordinary loss on the call he is writing, his position should be established at the end of an intermediate decline in a bull market as defined in the price behavior chapter. If, instead, he prefers to write calls against a long-term holding which he prefers not to sell, the ideal time to write calls is at the end of an intermediate advance in a bull market so that the call premiums stand the greatest chance of being collected. If the call writer is so disposed and is working with stock that is so low priced that it will probably never be sold, thus incurring capital gains taxes, the investor has the flexibility of writing calls at the end of intermediate rallies in both bull markets and bear markets. This is only true in this case because falling stock prices in a bear market are immaterial, the major objective being to collect call premiums. Where timing of establishing and closing of transactions is important, the timing tools presented in the chapter on high risk/high reward strategies should prove especially helpful.

3. In all cases it is desirable to write calls with premiums above fair value as determined by the pricing curves presented in the chapter on pricing. As a rule of thumb, pre-

miums should be at least 25 percent greater than fair value.

The final strategy to be covered under the moderate risk/moderate reward category is the short stock—sell put strategy. This approach is ideally applied in a bear market in which the investor hopes to augment his short profits with the collection of put premiums, while at the same time affording himself the protection of the put premiums collected in case the stock is at or above the strike price at the expiration date. Again the medium of numerical examples will be used to demonstrate the four possible outcomes of this strategy. The Bethlehem Steel example just used for the buy stock—write call strategy will be adapted, assuming that the premiums used in those examples can now be thought of as put premiums.

A. Stock Is Up— Position Closed Out at a Loss

Date	Action	Debit	Credit
June 1	Short 1,000 BS @ 29¼....................		$29,250
	Less commissions............................		($ 363)
June 1	Sell 10 puts BS @ 30 expiring Jan 31 for		
	$400 each..............................		$ 4,000
	Less commissions..........................		($ 118)

On November 1, the stock is trading at 34 and the investor decides to close out his positions.

	Debit	
Buy 1,000 BS @ 34 plus commissions covering short..............................	$34,389	
Buying 10 puts BS @ 30 expiring Jan. 31, for $50 each............................	$ 500	
Plus commission...........................	$ 50	

Return on Investment Calculation

Proceeds...................................	$28,887	(29,250 − 363)
Plus premium..............................	3,882	(4,000 − 118)
	$32,769	
Less cost of stock..........................	$34,389	(34,000 + 389)
Capital loss (short-term)....................	($ 1,620)	
Less closing cost of options.................	$ 550	(500 + 50)
Total loss.................................	$ 2,170	

$$\text{ROI} = \frac{\text{Total pretax loss}}{\text{Investment}} = \frac{-2170}{25,005} \times 100$$
$$= 8.7\% \text{ for 5 months}$$

B. Stock Down—
Puts Exercised

Date	Action	Debit	Credit
June 1			
	Short 1,000 BS @ 29¼....................		$29,250
	Less commissions.........................		($ 363)
June 1			
	Sell 10 puts BS @ 30 expiring January 31 for		
	$400 each.............................		$ 4,000
	Less commissions.........................		($ 118)

The stock drops gradually to 25 at the expiration date and the put buyer elects to exercise his put by delivering his stock to the put writer (our investor) at a price of 30.

January 31, 1974

The put writer purchases 1,000 BS @ 30, honoring the puts he wrote..............................	$30,000	
Plus commissions................................	$ 370	

Return on Investment Calculation

Proceeds...................................	$28,887	(29,250 − 363)
Plus premium..............................	3,882	(4,000 − 118)
	$32,769	
Less cost of stock..........................	$30,370	(30,000 + 370)
Ordinary income...........................	$ 2,399	

$$\text{ROI} = \frac{\text{Total pretax gain}}{\text{Investment}} = \frac{2,399}{25,005} \times 100$$
$$= 9.6\% \text{ in 8 months}$$

C. Stock Down—
Position Closed Out

Date	Action	Debit	Credit
June 1			
	Short 1,000 BS @ 29¼......................		$29,250
	Less commissions.........................		($ 363)
June 1			
	Sell 10 puts BS @ 30 expiring Jan. 31 for		
	$400 each................................		$ 4,000
	Less commissions		($ 118)

The stock drops sharply to 25 and the investor decides to close out his position.

August 1

Cover short of 1,000 shares BS @ 25..............	$25,000
Plus commissions................................	$ 336

August 1

Close out 10 puts BS @ 30 now trading for $700....	$ 7,000
Plus commissions................................	$ 145

Return on Investment Calculation

Proceeds.....................................	$28,887	(29,250 − 363)
Plus premium................................	$ 3,882	(4,000 − 118)
	$32,769	
Less cost of stock...........................	25,336	(25,000 + 336)
Less closing cost of puts....................	7,145	(7,000 + 145)
Profit....................................	$ 288	

$$\text{ROI} = \frac{\text{Total pretax gain}}{\text{Investment}} = \frac{288}{25,005} \times 100$$
$$= 1.2\% \text{ in 2 months}$$

Actually, with this small a profit, the investor probably would not be tempted to unwind the position. If, instead, the profit approached the maximum of $2,399 he would receive as in case B with the puts being exercised, the incentive would then be greater, especially if this occurred early in the option's life.

In this case the investor would simply collect the put premiums less commissions of $3,882 ($4,000 — $118) and probably write another put after the first one expired. In this case the return on investment would be

D. The Stock Remains Virtually Unchanged

$$\frac{\text{Total pretax gain}}{\text{Investment}} = \frac{\$\ 3,882}{\$25,005} \times 100$$
$$= 15.5\% \text{ in 8 months}$$

The short stock—write put strategy is very seldom employed, mainly because most option writers seem to be most comfortable with call writing fully hedged and attempt to do this regardless of the price environment they are in. In Bull Markets they make a lot of money and in Bear Markets they generally lose money. Their consolation may be that the premiums collected gave them a smaller loss than that suffered by someone who had simply purchased a stock, but the logical thing to do would have been to employ a bear market strategy.

The dynamics of the short stock—write put strategy are probably best demonstrated with the same type of diagram used for the buy stock —write call strategy. Figure 7–3 represents an example of a typical short stock—write put trade. This is compared with simply shorting stock. The profit profile of the put-writing strategy offers a maximum profit equal to the put premium for any price below the point where

FIGURE 7–3

Profit Comparison between Shorting 100 Shares of Stock versus Shorting the Stock and Writing a Put with a $500 Premium

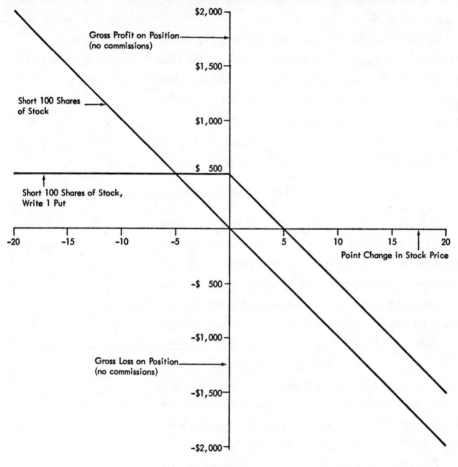

the position was established. Above that point the position loses ground at a rate of $100 per point of price increase until the point is reached at which the stock loss equals the put premiums, in our example, at a 5-point increase in the stock price. Again the relevant comparison with the short stock strategy is made by superimposing a probability distribution of likely prices. As with the call-writing example, an investor may ask why he should write a put, when he could make much more money simply shorting the stock. The answer is if one strives for consistently good results, the complement of a written put has to be superior for the large capitalization, cyclical stock traded on the CBOE. Otherwise, the investor is attempting the extreme case which is just not likely to occur. For the small capitalization company in extremis, that is another case entirely.

Another reason that call writers may tend to strictly write CBOE calls, when they have the alternative of puts, is that no dividends are received when writing puts. It may be painful to think of engaging in a policy which will not provide stock dividends, but the capital losses suffered in a bear market should more than make up for the difference.

Some rules that may be helpful in the short stock—write put strategy are the following:

1. Since the ideal environment for this strategy is a falling market, the strategy should be implemented in a bear market as defined by the market barometer.
2. The ideal time to implement the strategy is at the end of a rally in a bear market so that the chance of a move upwards against the position is at a minimum. For guidance, the methodology for recognizing such a point is covered in the chapter on price behavior. The time to close out positions is at

the end of intermediate declines or through expiration if the strike price is far above the market price with only a month until maturity.

3. The objective should be to write puts with premiums at least 25 percent greater than fair value as measured with the pricing graphs in Chapter 3, using 80 percent of the fair value of a call as an estimate for the put.

In all the foregoing moderate reward/moderate risk strategies no mention has been made of the amount of capital to be used. A suggested procedure is to think of the two stock trading strategies, shorting stock—buying puts as a gambling operation on a par with the buying of calls so that only risk capital which can be totally lost without affecting your life style or the ability to pay bills is utilized. Of that capital, a fully invested position should be diversified among five different underlying stock positions without using margin. This approach, following the buying and selling techniques recommended, should keep the investor out of trouble, both financially and emotionally.

The two option-writing strategies can be thought of as a way to earn a higher return than with bonds, but with somewhat greater risk of eroding your principal. Therefore the recommended procedure for an overall money management approach would be to have well over half of total capital in a savings account, in quality government, corporate, and possibly municipal bonds, with the remainder dedicated to an option-writing strategy appropriate to the current price environment.

Each individual will have to determine which, if any, of the strategies presented in this book he would be most comfortable in attempting. This will be determined not only by the amount of personal means, but mainly by the temperament, interest, and time available for each individual. The conclusion may even be to select a professional to manage part of your capital. Even in this case the knowledge of the techniques presented in this book should prove helpful.

The Moderate Reward/ Minimal Risk Strategies

8

The strategies presented in this chapter should provide the major source of acceptance for CBOE options as an important money management tool. The reason for this is the simple truth that herein lies the key to consistently successful results in the stock market. No other strategies offer the same management of risk, while providing a very satisfactory return on invested capital. No other approach works as scientifically with the way stock prices truly behave. Rather than attempting to forecast a future price level, which no one has demonstrated publicly that he can do with any consistency, these strategies work with price ranges and the expected percent change in price which can reasonably occur during a specific time period. Such things can be measured at least in terms of probabilities and allowed for in the application of a strategy. Another relationship which can be well defined is the behavior of a particular CBOE option relative to its underlying stock. The best work in the field has been done by Fisher Black and Myron Scholes,[1] but

---

[1] F. Black and M. Scholes, "The Pricing of Options and Corporate Liabilities," *Journal of Political Economy*, vol. 81, no. 3, May/June 1973.

their mathematics is well above the heads of even the most astute Wall Street professionals. What they essentially did was to define the behavior of an arbitrage between stock purchased and call options in the same stock sold (written). This arbitrage concept is the heart of this chapter. Arbitrage is defined as the simultaneous purchase and sale of the same or equivalent security in order to profit from price discrepancies. Perhaps the best means of presenting the benefits of a stock-option arbitrage is to examine the graphs in Figures 8–1 and 8–2.

The first graph depicts the typical buy stock strategy, in this case for 100 shares of Upjohn. The prices shown actually occurred. The area covered by parallel lines represents the loss area for the stock, which begins below the purchase price of $93\frac{1}{4}$. There is only one direction for the price to move to realize a profit, up. This is the basic buy-and-keep-your-fingers-crossed strategy employed every day in the stock market, very often with little success.

The second graph presents the profit and loss picture for a partial hedge strategy. This position consists of 100 shares of Upjohn stock purchased at $93\frac{1}{4}$ a share, combined with the sale of three Upjohn July calls with a strike price of $100. The premium for each call is $1,350. Now, rather than there being a loss if the stock drops below $93\frac{1}{4}$, the stock has to drop *below* $52\frac{3}{4}$ to cause a loss or rise *above* $123\frac{5}{8}$. In other words the position is protected above *and* below the price paid for the stock. The stock position is embedded in a profit zone. How does

FIGURE 8–1

Unprotected Stock Purchase

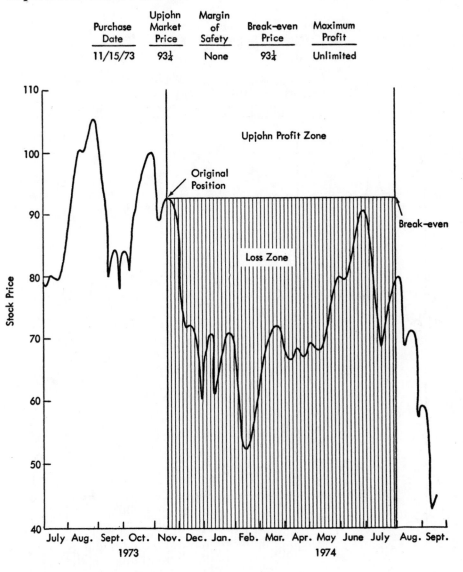

Purchase Date	Upjohn Market Price	Margin of Safety	Break-even Price	Maximum Profit
11/15/73	93¼	None	93¼	Unlimited

FIGURE 8–2

Partial Hedge Strategy

Date	Upjohn Market Price	Option Sold	Premium Received	Upper Protection	Lower Protection	Maximum Profit
11/15/73	93¼	July 100's	$1,350	123 5/8	52 3/4	89.5% in 8½ Months

Strategy { Sell 3 Upjohn Calls, July 100's @ $1,350 Each
Buy 100 Shares Upjohn @ 93¼ }

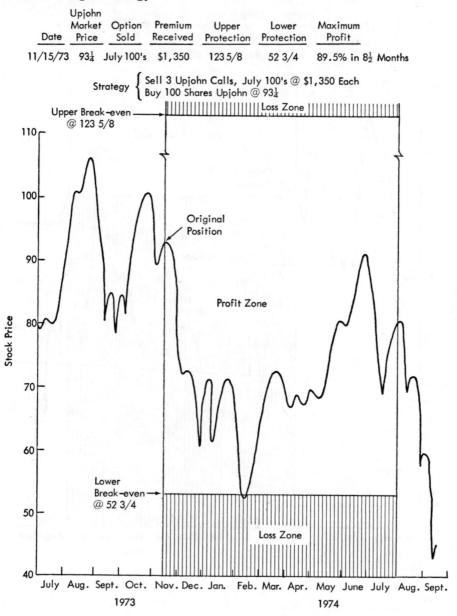

this occur? If the stock remains at or below the strike price of 100 at the expiration date, the call premiums will be collected. Since they would offset any decline in the stock's price, the lower breakeven is at the point where the loss in the stock's value equals the premiums collected. In this case the total premiums collected are $4,050 to be offset against 100 shares of stock, for a protection of $40\frac{1}{2}$ points.

The upper breakeven level is determined by a different means. As the stock rises in price the position gains on the increase in stock price but loses on the calls that are short until the point that the short loss overtakes the increase in the stock value plus the premiums collected. This is the upper breakeven level and can be determined both graphically and numerically, as we shall later see.

The key to understanding these arbitrage strategies lies in studying how option premiums change relative to the underlying stock, as well as the relationship between the strike price of the option and the current stock price, the volatility of the underlying stock price, the time remaining in the option's life, and the level of interest rates. Although this may appear to be a frightening array of relationships, it is possible to encapsulate them in a graph usually called the standard warrant diagram. Such diagrams are presented in Figures 8–3 to 8–7 for the five levels of volatility found in CBOE stocks.

In order to standardize the information as much as possible, the option premiums and stock prices are expressed as a ratio by dividing each

FIGURE 8-3
CBOE Analog of the Standard Warrant Diagram: Volatility—10 Percent

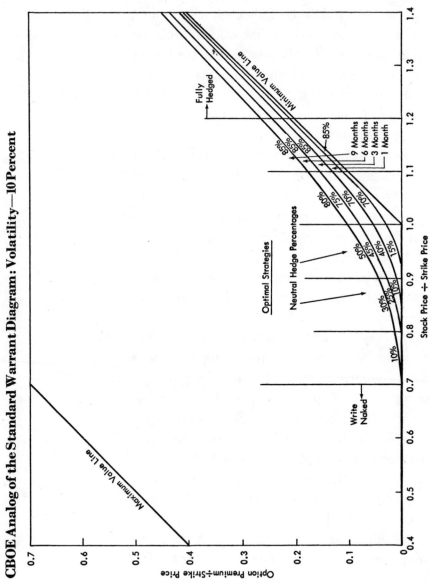

FIGURE 8-4

CBOE Analog of the Standard Warrant Diagram: Volatility—20 Percent

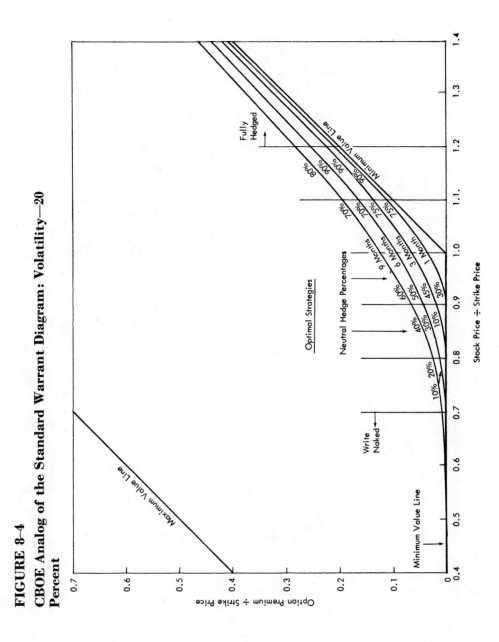

FIGURE 8-5
CBOE Analog of the Standard Warrant Diagram: Volatility—30 Percent

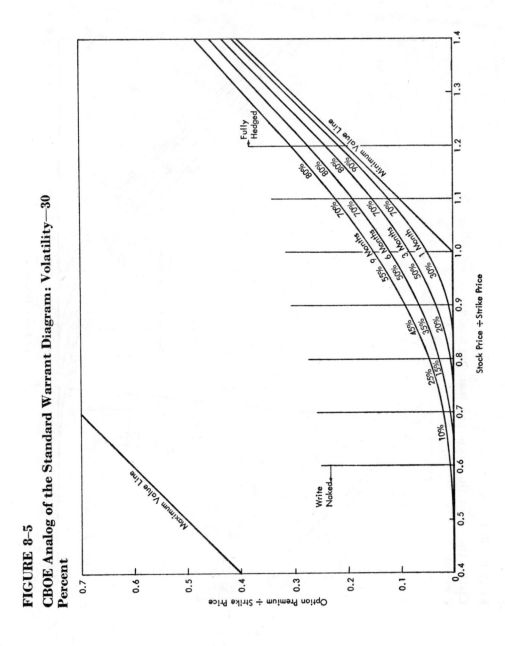

FIGURE 8-6

CBOE Analog of the Standard Warrant Diagram: Volatility—40 Percent

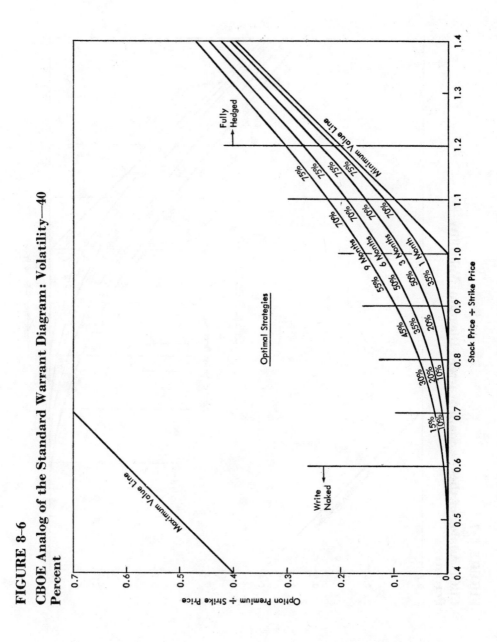

FIGURE 8-7

CBOE Analog of the Standard Warrant Diagram: Volatility—50 Percent

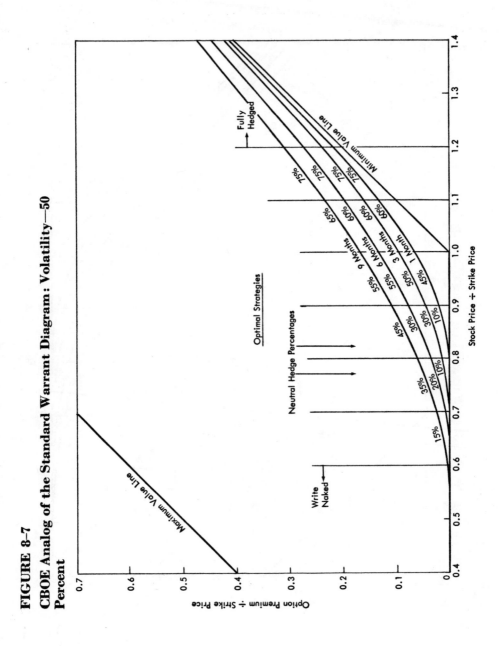

by the strike price of the option. If the stock price were trading exactly at the strike price of the option, the ratio would be 1.0 along the horizontal axis of the graph. The option premium expressed as a fraction of the option's strike price is plotted along the vertical axis. If an option had a premium of $1,000 and a strike price of 100, the ratio would be 0.1.

The values which an option premium can exhibit range between a theoretical maximum of equalling the price of the stock down to the cash value of the option at the expiration date. This minimum holds true because an option to buy 100 shares of stock at $100 a share is worth at least $500 less commission costs, if the stock is trading at $105 on the day the call options expire. Looking at the first standard warrant diagram, Figure 8–3, with 10-percent volatility, the maximum value line starts at a value of 0.4 and moves upward at a 45-degree angle so that at 0.5 on the option scale it corresponds with 0.5 on the stock scale. In actual practice option values tend to approximate the minimum value line, which runs along the bottom of the graph at a value of zero from readings of 0.4 on the stock price/strike price scale all the way up to 1.0. Above 1.0, the minimal value line begins to rise at a 45-degree angle so that each point equals the in-money value of the option. The price curves which relate the option premium to the underlying stock are derived from the premium curves presented in the chapter on the CBOE. Time on this diagram runs from the nine-month curve down to the minimum value line and demonstrates quite clearly the fact that a given option with the same strike price and underlying stock price as one with less time is worth more. For instance, on the 10-percent volatility graph at the stock price equals the strike price ratio 1.0, a nine-month option would have a premium of 0.1 of the strike price value of the stock ($1,000 if the strike price were $100), a six-month option would have a premium of $750, a three-month $500, and a one-month $250.

Actually the most important measurements which can be derived from the diagram are the degree of change in option premium for a point change in the underlying stock price and the upper and lower breakeven levels for any given ratio of options short in a position relative to stock owned. The slope of the various curves measures the degree of option premium change with a one-point change in the underlying stock. In the 10-percent volatility graph, Figure 8–3, the nine-month maturity line has an almost flat slope below a stock price/strike price ratio of 0.7, then gradually increases its slope until above a stock price/strike price ratio of 1.2, where the slope approaches a value of 1.0 or 45 degrees, equal to that of the minimum value line. In fact, the small numbers above the graph give the value of the slope over a narrow range starting at 10 percent and ranging up to 85 percent. We will come back to these important numbers in a short while. The second important measure, the upper and lower breakeven levels, is obtained by running a line from any given

point on the curve upwards at the same slope as
the curve at the starting point until the minimum
value line is intersected above a value of 1.0.
This is the upper breakeven level for the arbitrage being measured. Running the same line
down to the left until it intersects the minimal
value line running along the bottom of the
graph below a level of stock price/strike price
of 1.0, gives the lower breakeven level of a given
arbitrage. As an example, let's suppose that a
given nine-month option with 10 percent volatility has an option premium divided by strike
price of .075 and the underlying stock is trading
at its strike price of $100 per share. As the ex-
ample in Figure 8–8 shows, the slope of the
price curve is 50 percent. What this means is
that any movement in the underlying stock price
near this point would shift the option premium
by only half as much. Therefore, an arbitrage
established with ten calls short, representing
1,000 shares of stock, and 500 shares of stock
long would not change in value for small stock
price changes around this point. If a line is
drawn through this point with a slope of $\frac{1}{2}$ and
extended upward to the upward sloping mini-
mum value line, the value of the intersection is
1.2. This is where the position would be if it had
a zero profit on the expiration date of the options. For our 100 strike price, this would trans-
late into $120 a share for the stock. If the same
line is extended downward to the left it hits the
horizontal segment of the minimal value line at
0.82. This would be the value of the stock price
which would also yield a zero profit at expira-

FIGURE 8-8
CBOE Analog of the Standard Warrant Diagram: Volatility—10 Percent

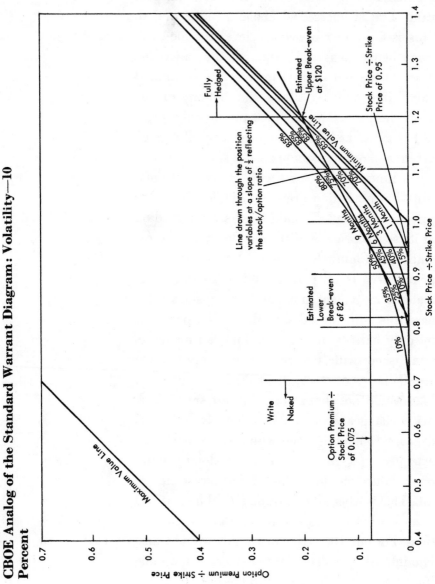

tion date and equals $82 in our case. Anywhere between $82 and $120 at the expiration date, the position will make a profit.

Perhaps the reader has a hint what this can mean for money management. The gist of it is that the standard diagram can be used to design an arbitrage position which will suffer no potential loss for small price moves away from the original stock price and will return a profit at expiration date within a 20-percent range above and below the current stock price. Since the price curves are relatively fixed, a position can be totally designed before it is established. If a range of 82 to 120 does not seem appropriate, the option/stock ratio can be adjusted so that a different set of breakeven levels results.

At this stage the next logical step in the explanation is to investigate how the upper and lower breakeven levels can be determined numerically and how the profit potential for each position can be determined as well. The simplest and yet most versatile means of determining the upper and lower breakeven levels is with "tee" account analysis. Such bookkeeping entries are identical to the entires made for various transactions in the monthly account statement provided by most brokerage firms.

Let's use our example of a stock with a price of $100 a share, let's call it XYZ Corp., and have a nine-month call option with a strike price of $100 trading at $750 each. If our standard curves indicate an ideal position of ten calls short and 500 shares of stock long, our T-account entries would be as follows:

1. Purchase 500 shares of XYZ Corp. at 96 for 500 × $96 or $48,000. The entry would be:

Debit	Credit
1. $48,000	

2. Sell 10 XYZ call options maturing in nine months for $750 each for a positive cash flow in the account of $7,500. The entry would be:

Debit	Credit
1. $48,000	2. $7,500

3. By selling ten calls, the writer is now obligated to deliver 1,000 shares of XYZ Corp. stock at a price of $100 to honor the calls, or a total obligation of $100,000. The entry to reflect this is:

Debit	Credit
1. $48,000	2. $ 7,500
	3. 100,000

Netting out the account, the investor finds himself with a net credit of $59,500.

Debit	Credit
1. $48,000	2. $ 7,500
	3. 100,000
	$107,500
	−48,000
	$ 59,500

This amount is the extent of the open obligation the investor has by owning only 500 shares of XYZ Corp. stock to honor a 1,000-share obligation at $100 a share. If the 500 shares he is net short were to be acquired for $59,500, the deficit in the account, the overall position would break even. By dividing the $59,500 by 500 shares, the result of $119 a share is obtained as the breakeven price. This compares with our graphical estimate of $120.

If the stock prices remains at or below $100 a share at the expiration date, the obligation to deliver 1,000 shares of XYZ Corp at $100 is removed. The T-account would look like this:

Debit	Credit
1. $48,000	2. $ 7,500
	3. ~~$100,000~~

or

Debit	Credit
1. 48,000	2. $ 7,500

Since the premiums will be kept at or below $100, the $7,500 acts as an offset against any loss in the 500 shares of stock purchased at 96. The figure of $48,000 minus $7,500, or $40,-500, could be attained for the stock and the position would break even. The amount $40,500 divided by 500 equals $81, providing the lower breakeven price. Another way to arrive at the same number is to divide the premiums collected by 500 shares, or $7,500 divided by 500 shares, for 15 points of protection. Subtracting this from 96 yields the lower breakeven of $81.

The reason for introducing the tee account approach is that it is the most general and easily adaptable to complex positions. If stock is purchased at many different prices, the total dollar value would still appear on the left-hand side of the tee account. The total premiums would appear in the right-hand side along with the total dollar value of the delivery obligation of all the calls that are short. The upper breakeven point would still be obtained by netting out the overall position and dividing the difference between the left-hand and the right-hand sides by the net amount of stock short in the position. The lower breakeven would be determined by dividing the number of shares in the long position into the total premium income possible and obtaining the points of protection for the position. Subtracting this number from the average cost per share of the long position provides the lower breakeven level.

Computing the maximum profit level for the position is the other important variable to determine. The maximum profit level is attained at the strike price of the short options in the position. This occurs because at this point the best price possible is obtained for the long stock, while one still collects all the premiums written. Therefore to compute the maximum profit possible one simply adds the profits gained by the long stock's moving up to the strike price to the dollar value of the premiums collected. In our case this would be 500 shares times (100 —

96) $= 4$ or \$2,000 plus the total premium income of \$7,500 for a grand total of \$9,500. To compute this as a return on capital simply divide this number by the dollars needed to purchase the long stock less the premiums on the

FIGURE 8–9

The Profit Profile

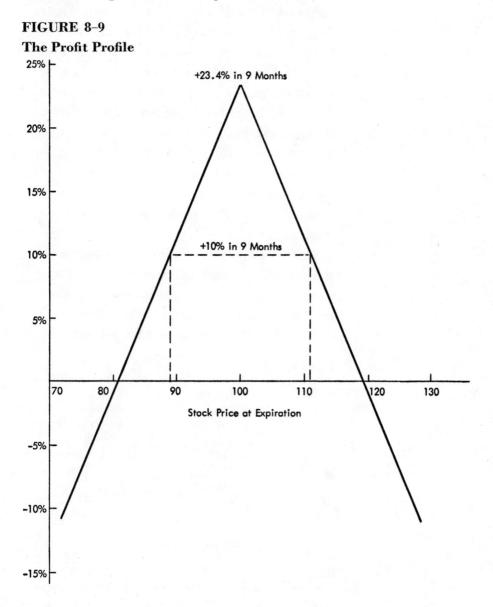

short calls. In our case this would be $48,000 less $7,500 and divided into $9,500 would yield a 23.4 percent pretax return for nine months.

The profit profile for the arbitrage thus assumes the shape of a triangle as shown in Figure 8–9, with the apex at the strike price of 100. Interestingly, even if the stock closes as low as 90 or as high as 112 at the expiration date, the return on capital is 10 percent in nine months. Not a bad target for a medium as imprecise as the stock market. If this were a more complex position one could perform the same analysis using the weighted average strike price for all the options in the position along with the tee account method for computing the breakeven levels.

The flexibility of designing the hedge position can probably be best appreciated by computing a range of breakeven levels for our XYZ Corp. position for a full range of hedge values. Table 8–1 presents this analysis with the percent hedge

TABLE 8–1

Hedge (percent)	Upper Breakeven	Lower Breakeven
0	107½	Profit of $7,500
10	108¾	21
20	110⅜	58½
30	112⅜	71
40	115⅛	77¼
50	119	81
60	124¾	83½
70	134¼	85¼
80	153½	86⅝
90	211	87⅝
100	00	88½

convention indicating how much stock is owned relative to the short options in the position. The incredible result is that the position can be made to realize a profit for a stock price ranging from zero to infinity. Of course the catch is that if an extreme position had to be properly adjusted by either totally covering the outstanding calls to protect a large price rise, or writing enough calls to buy enough downside protection a near infinite amount of funds would be required. Nonetheless, the degree of flexibility is amazing.

Now that virtually all the parameters have been covered, how does one go about designing a position? The first question to answer is, which option should I write? The answer is obtained by scanning the available option premiums, preferably with large premiums in terms of fair value. A good "write" as it is called would be two- to four-month options with premiums at least 25 percent above fair value as determined by the pricing curves in the chapter on pricing. Also to be considered is the nature of the fundamentals of the underlying stock. A stable company with solid fundamentals should be the candidate. The next question is how much of a hedge to establish. This is estimated roughly by entering the appropriate standard curve for the correct level of volatility and the current premium level and stock price combination. The recommended hedge is provided by the numbers on the curve closest to the point determined by the option premium and stock price. With this as a guide, the next question is, how much protection do I need? To provide this answer, a set of curves was generated, Figures 8–10 and 8–11, which portray the largest percentage down moves recorded for the ten years through June 30, 1974, for the different levels of volatility

FIGURE 8–10

Volatility versus Maximum Percentage Up Moves

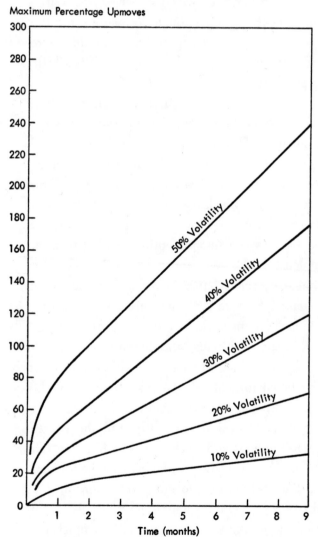

Maximum Percentage Upmoves

FIGURE 8–11

Volatility versus Maximum Percentage Down Moves

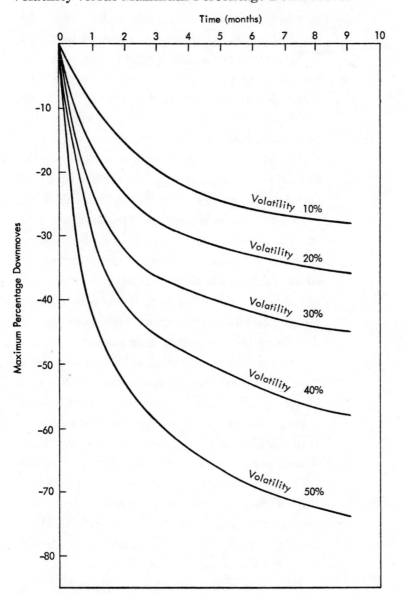

found on the CBOE. Since these curves give the maximum percent increases or decreases, they should yield safe breakeven levels. Once the breakeven level protection has been determined from these graphs, the percent hedge can be modified away from the neutral posture recommended with the standard curves. It is these breakeven levels which should determine the percent hedge. This can probably best be estimated by use of a ruler to test various sloped lines through a position point on the standard curve until the desired breakeven levels have been attained. This approximate slope, whether $\frac{1}{5}$, $\frac{1}{4}$, or whatever it may be, can be used to compute the actual breakevens using the tee account analysis for the final check. In case it is not possible to bracket both levels with a given hedge percentage, the upper breakeven should determine the hedge in a bear market.

The other cross check should be a computation of the maximum percent return, with a suggested cutoff of a minimum 40 percent annual pretax return on invested capital. The next step is to establish five to ten equally sized positions. A time period of two to four months is suggested because the breakeven levels are reasonable. Beyond this time period, the span of the breakeven levels would have to be too wide to allow for the maximum expected range in the underlying stock's price.

How should the positions be managed? The simplistic approach is to establish the widest breakeven limits possible and just allow the position to remain unadjusted for the life of the options. The risk is that occasionally one of the breakeven levels will be threatened and the level can then be either adjusted further away, or the position closed out. Another approach, which is preferred by the computer-oriented investors, is to establish filter levels, such as every 5 percent change in the underlying stock, where another 100 shares of stock is purchased if the stock is rising in price or another call is written if the stock is falling in price. In general, the most effective way to manage the positions is with a day-to-day monitoring of each position by tracking the price level of the underlying stock, the changes in the premium levels and the up-to-date profit and loss for both the stock and option sides of the arbitrage. The most sensible management of money comes from making small adjustments in response to day-to-day changes in the market. If the market begins to weaken, all breakeven levels should be reviewed to see whether more downside protection is needed. If the full protection dictated by the maximum price change curves was not initially set up, the position can be adjusted to a point near or actually encompassing this extreme level. This is the art of the method. Experience will teach how much to adjust, but several guidelines can be followed to aid in the decision making process.

1. The maximum profit attainable for each hedge position should be computed so that the position can be closed out in case this level is approximated before the options expire.

2. Any adjustments made in the hedges should be accomplished by either buying more stock or writing more calls, rather than taking losses by selling out stock to increase the ratio of calls to stock, or buying back calls at a loss to increase the percent hedge.

3. When establishing a position one should take a moderate posture, usually ranging from a 30-percent to a 60-percent hedge. In this way severe adjustments are avoided in case the stock changes direction radically. It is recommended that 30 percent of available funds be invested in 90-day treasury bills in case added buying power is needed to purchase stock for adjustment purposes.

4. The philosophy of the partial hedge should be to attempt to let the options expire with the stock price as close to the maximum profit level as possible, providing enough breakeven level protection so that the risk of a loss is kept to a minimum, and capitalizing on any profit opportunities which arise from unexpected price changes.

5. The only way that market judgment is used is to recognize when an extreme move has occurred in the market and take the resulting profits, while moderating any extreme postures which could be hurt by a sharp reversal of prices.

6. Operating the hedges in the recommended manner will allow a great deal of tax management opportunities to occur. If a rally in prices takes place, positions can be closed out with an eye toward taking a capital gain

on the stock side of the hedge, while establishing an ordinary loss on the short call side. This will theoretically permit an investor to pay all of his income taxes on a capital gains basis. All the ordinary losses will be used to offset any salary or dividend income.

While the partial hedge approach just discussed attempts to capture the maximum profits available from an arbitrage between long stock and short calls, the neutral hedge is a variation which attempts to capture overvalued call premiums without managing breakeven levels or closing out positions at market turns. The essence of the neutral hedge is to have no feeling whatsoever of future price directions. The mechanics of the method are to search for overvalued premiums as determined by the option pricing curves of Chapter 3. The initial percent hedge established is determined by entering the standard warrant diagram and reading the recommended percent hedge from the curves. Once this hedge is established it is adjusted only as dictated by the percentages on the curve. If a 30-percent hedge was the initial position—for example, 300 shares of stock purchased and 10 calls sold—and the slope on the curves called for a 40-percent hedge, another 100 shares of stock would be purchased. If the curves called for a 20-percent hedge, 100 shares of stock would be sold. Because so much adjusting is required, the guideline of always adding to a position to adjust as in the partial hedge has to be ignored, for otherwise the position would become too large for the available capital. As the stock moves higher in price a fatter hedge is called for, which means selling some calls usually at a loss. If the stock price moves lower a smaller hedge is called for, which means selling some stock, usually at a loss. Over time, the process tends to yield a profit as overvalued calls become less overvalued and are therefore closed out at a gain in the constant adjustment process.

As one might imagine, this strategy, while requiring no market judgment whatsoever, demands constant monitoring to the point of watching prices sometimes from minute to minute. The costs of the transactions (brokerage commissions, fees and taxes) are prohibitive, which relegates this approach to a member of the CBOE or other appropriate options exchange.

A somewhat less flexible approach than the partial hedge, but requiring far less capital, is a technique called spreading. Essentially the method is to buy a call as a substitute for purchasing stock in an arbitrage. There are many variations on this basic theme, but one very sensible one will be presented. The procedure is to look for a pair of options in a given underlying stock that have the same expiration dates, but different strike prices, where the premium of the lower strike price option is twice that of the higher strike price option. An actual example which existed in April, 1974, with Atlantic Richfield calls, were the October 90s trading at $600 and the October 100s trading at $337.50. The recommended hedge is 33 percent for several reasons, the first one being a positive cash flow for the position. The three calls sold would provide $1012.50 in premiums deposited in the account, while the call purchased would cause a cash drain of $600. This net cash flow is important because, if the stock remained at or below 100 until the expiration date, that amount of $1012.50 minus $600 or $412.50 would be the gross profit for the position. In fact, even if the stock dropped to zero, this amount would be the gross profit for the position. There is no downside risk. If the options were to expire with the stock above 90, the long option would be worth the in-money value or $100 for each point above 90. The maximum profit in the position would be attained at a price of 100, at which the investor would enjoy $1,000 for his one long call and collect $1012.50 in premiums for his short calls. This total of $2,012.50 less the cost of the long call, $600, would yield a profit of $1,412.50. Above a price of 100, the position would begin eroding by $200 per point rise because of the 200 shares net short in the option position. The gross profit of $1,412.50 would finally be overcome if the stock rose above $107\frac{1}{8}$. This is the upper breakeven point. Since the stock at the time of the trade was 86, the position had unlimited downside protection and 21 points' protection on the upside. The actual margin requirements for the trade, using New York Stock Exchange rules were as follows:

1. Purchase one call October Atlantic Richfield 90 for $600. Cash required $600.
2. Sell three calls October Atlantic Richfield

100s for 3⅜ each. The margin requirement for each call is:

a. Thirty percent of the market value of the stock = 0.3 × $8,600 = $2,580.

b. Less the premium of the option sold or $337.50, reducing the $2,580 to $2,242.50.

c. Less the mark to the market of the short call or 100 − 86 = $1,400, further reducing the margin requirement to $842.50. For the three calls this amounts to $2,527.50.[1]

Therefore total cash required in the account is $2,527.50 + $600 or $3,127.50, if no marginable stock is available to cover the three short calls. For this, there is an opportunity to make $1,412.50 in six months for a 45.2 percent pretax return on capital.

There are many ways to handle the spread position. The simplest approach is to remain with the position until the options expire, closing it out if the position reaches a predetermined loss prior to expiration. The predetermined loss should be less than 20 percent of the margin required for the hedge. The more active approach involves market timing and judgment in line with the work in the chapter on trading techniques. In this case the spread is established at a perceived market turn. If an expected rally occurs, the spread trader "lifts the leg" and closes out the protective short call, thus convert-

---

[1] New uniform margin rules in effect after February, 1975 would only require $1,957.50. See Chapter 9 for a further explanation.

ing the spread into a long call trade. This should only be done at the end of intermediate declines in a bull market and with options having at least two months of life. The beauty of the method is there is no downside risk if it is done correctly, allowing the trader to establish his position on weakness, yet protect himself from being early.

The opposite approach to trading with spreads is to establish a position at the end of a rally in a bear market. Upon receipt of evidence that the expected decline is beginning, the long call leg is closed out and the short call allowed to ride with the decline. In this manner the short trade is given a large amount of upside protection in case the trade is established early, yet allows the trader to attempt a high price level for his short call. The most popular use of spreads will undoubtably occur as more and more sophisticated investors take advantage of the favorable tax ruling offered CBOE traders. Although the technique should be practiced only at intermediate declines in bull markets, a spread could be established between calls in a given stock with more than six months to maturity in the long call with the lower strike price, and less than six months in the higher strike price. If the rally occurs, the investor faces the prospect of a long-term capital gain in his long call and a smaller ordinary loss in his short call, which enjoys ordinary tax treatment. In this manner, the investor provides himself with a safe, low-cost means of paying most or all of his taxes on a long-term capital gains basis having offset the ordinary losses against his salary. And, in case the rally begins to change direction before the six months have elapsed, the trader can close out his short call for the ordinary loss and write a new call to lock in the profit in the long call. The end result may be a smaller capital gain if the stock price does decline, but the economic gain can be maintained with the offsetting profit in the new short calls. The variations are nearly infinite. However, the true benefit of spreading is the large flexibility in strategies and maneuverability that can be obtained for a small amount of capital. For the aspiring option investor this is undoubtably the best and safest training ground.

The fourth arbitrage strategy is the writing of puts, coupled with the shorting of stock. However, this is not a true reciprocal of the partial hedge approach using calls. For one thing the put premiums, when they are available, should be less than premiums for calls. Secondly, there will be no dividends available on puts. Finally, the problems of borrowing stock to go short on a large scale, as well as the mechanics of needing upticks to establish short positions, make the technique unwieldy. Add to this the sharpness of short-covering rallies in a bear market, which will cause tremendous scrambling to adjust breakeven levels. And, as if this were not enough, an entire new set of standard option premium/stock prices curves would have to be developed in order to determine proper percent hedges. In a grand economic sense, this approach should be destined to play fourth fiddle to the partial hedge using calls.

Taxes, Margin and Record Keeping

9

The key to consistent profits with options is money management, and this includes knowledge of tax laws, margin regulations, and proper record keeping. The tax rules applicable to CBOE options apply only to call options, since trading in puts and straddles has not been authorized as of the writing of this book. An individual dealing in call options is either a holder (a buyer) or a writer (a seller). The holder of an option is considered to own a capital asset with a cost basis established at the date of purchase and a holding period which commences on that same date. Three events can occur to the capital asset. It can either be exercised, sold, or allowed to expire.

1. If the option is exercised, the holder becomes the owner of the underlying stock. The cost basis for tax purposes is the sum of the cost of exercising the option plus the purchase cost of the option itself. The holding period for the stock begins with the exercise date and *does not* include the holding period of the call.

2. If the call is sold, the holder receives either

a capital gain or a loss determined by comparing the proceeds of the sale with the cost basis of the call. The holding period is determined by the holding period of the call. A long-term period is more than six months —short-term six months or less.

3. If the call expires unexercised, the loss is a capital loss equal to the cost basis of the call. The loss is considered long term or short term depending on the holding period from the acquisition date until expiration.

The call holder's tax strategy should ideally be to achieve long-term capital gains and short-term losses. If the holder of a call decides to exercise, he does not incur a tax based on the exercise, but he should take care to recognize that the holding period of the stock acquired through exercise begins on the exercise date. If the call had been held more than six months before exercise and was profitable, it may be more advantageous to sell the call and realize a long-term capital gain. If not, the cost basis of the exercise stock will be the exercise price plus the cost of the call, making it very difficult to achieve a long-term gain from this higher cost basis.

If the call has declined in value, the holder may wish to sell it before it has been held for more than six months to realize a short-term loss. The advantage is that short-term losses can be offset against both long-term and short-term gains in any given tax year, while long-term losses can be offset only against long-term capital gains or offset against ordinary income at the maximum rate of $1,000 per year with the $1,000 writeoff representing $2,000 worth of loss.

If the call has any value because the stock is selling above the exercise price, but is worth less than the cost basis of the call, the holder of a long-term position can convert this into a short-term loss by exercising the call and immediately selling the stock. The disadvantage of this strategy is the cost of two full stock commissions, one incurred on the exercise of the call and the other on the sale of the stock. If the added expense is less than the tax benefit, it is a worthwhile strategy.

If an investor owns stock long term with a profit and desires to lock in the profit without avoiding the benefit of further price appreciation, he can do so by purchasing a call and selling short an equivalent amount of the stock. Since it has been ruled that a call is not substantially identical with the stock, this route is available without jeopardizing the holding period of the long stock. The investor unwinds his position by exercising his call to cover the short stock, selling the original long stock for a long-term capital gain. While the short-sale rules would require that the loss on closing the short sale is a long-term capital loss, this would be limited to the difference between the short-sale price and the exercise price of the call. The loss would mainly equal the cost of the call.

If the long stock had declined after the short-sale–buy-call transaction, the investor would deliver his long stock to close the short-stock position, thus realizing a long-term capital gain on the long stock. The call could be sold for a loss, which would be short term depending on the holding period of the call. The short-sale rules do not apply to the call in this case, since it is ruled not to be substantially identical to the long stock.

The acquisition of a call falls under the wash-sale rules if an investor sells underlying stock at a loss during the wash sale period determined by the purchase of the call. This period extends for 30 days before the call purchase, includes the purchase date, and 30 days after the purchase. The loss incurred by the sale of the underlying stock during the wash sale period will be disallowed. If the call is exercised, the sale basis of the stock acquired through the exercise is that of the stock sold during the wash sale period, adjusted for any difference between the proceeds in the wash sale and the cost of the new stock, which includes the call premium and the cost of exercise. The holding period of the new stock acquired in the exercise includes the holding period of the wash-sale stock. The holding period of the call has no effect.

There is no provision in the IRS Code or in the regulations for the subsequent allowance of the wash-sale loss if the call is not exercised. In the opinion of Oppenheim, Appel, Dixon & Co., New York, the wash-sale loss would be allowed on the date of expiration or sale of the call. They anticipate that the holding period of the call would have added on to it the holding period of the stock involved in the wash sale. Thus, if the holding period of the wash-sale stock had been long term, the deferred loss would be ruled long term even if the call had been held less than six months.

The writer (seller) of calls receives radically different tax treatment than the buyer of calls. This occurs because the writer's obligation to deliver underlying stock upon exercise is considered a liability and not an asset. The tax treatment of the consideration for assuming that risk, known as the premium, is held in limbo until termination of the contractual obligation, whether through exercise, expiration, or a closing purchase transaction. The three cases are treated as follows:

1. The exercise transaction is initiated by the holder of the call, not the writer. When the writer delivers stock on exercise against the strike price of the call, he realizes a capital gain or loss. He treats the transaction as a sale of the stock he delivers. The premium which had been held in suspense until completion of the contractual obligation is included as part of the proceeds of the sale. For tax purposes, the total proceeds of the sale, the premium income plus the payment at the exercise price, are compared with the cost basis of the stock delivered to determine the amount of gain or loss. The holding period of the stock delivered determines whether the gain or loss is long or short term.

2. If the holder of the call allows it to expire

unexercised, the writer treats the premium received as ordinary income, which is realized upon the expiration date.

3. The writer has the opportunity to terminate his contractual obligation by initiating a closing purchase transaction. To accomplish this he purchases an equivalent call, designating it a closing transaction. In doing this he realizes either ordinary income or ordinary loss, measured by the proceeds from the premium originally received less the cost of the closing purchase.

In writing calls, the writer has a great deal of latitude in determining whether he will be taxed on an ordinary or a capital gains basis. For this reason, the writer has more tax strategies open to him than the call buyer. The first part of the writer's strategy is to determine whether he should write naked or covered, meaning whether he should own the stock he is writing against or not. Writing naked, naturally, is writing without owning the underlying stock.

Writing naked is basically a more leveraged and protected way to trade stock on the short side. If the stock declines, the writer can either establish a profit through a closing purchase or allow the call to expire unexercised. If the stock begins to rise in price, the writer can elect to close out his position with a purchase, to acquire a call thus establishing a spread, or to purchase stock to cover his exercise obligation. Acquiring stock puts his tax status in the same position as if he had originally written on a covered basis. Acquiring a call may lead to tax questions which have not yet received IRS rulings.

While the exercise of a call is not controlled by the option writer, he can assume that in the vast majority of cases an option will be exercised only on the final day allowable prior to expiration. Economics determines that this is so. A holder of a profitable call has to come up with at least the money required under current margin regulations to take possession of the stock being purchased through exercise. If the holder can simply sell a profitable call without having to put up the extra money or to pay the larger commissions required to exercise, why should he take the more costly route? He may do so if he had originally purchased a call while waiting to receive extra funds and now wants to put those funds to use by purchasing the stock through an exercise, but, again, this is an exception. The great majority of call buyers are traders, not investors.

Determination of the specific writer who will be chosen to exercise depends first on a random selection of a Clearing Corporation member by the CBOE, then on a random selection of a particular account by the member firm. When the writer wrote the call or whether or not he has covered the call with a stock purchase has no bearing on the selection process. It's a safe assumption that if a call is trading in the money in the final days of an option's life, the option will be exercised. At least the risk is great enough in the final days that the writer should assume that exercise will occur.

If an option is exercised before the establishment of a six-month holding period, the writer can protect his long stock by purchasing new stock on a cash basis for delivery against the option, while writing a new call against his original long stock. In this case, if the stock continued to rise and the position became long term, the writer would realize a long-term capital gain on his original long stock, a short-term capital loss on the stock purchased on a cash basis to honor the exercise, and an ordinary loss on the closing purchase of the second call when the entire position was unwound. The one tax complication in this procedure might occur if the second 100 shares of stock purchased to honor the exercise was done on a regular way trade. As such it might be ruled as a short sale, thus jeopardizing the holding period of the original long stock.

At all times the buyer or writer of CBOE options should be careful about purchases and sales of the underlying stock in that they may fall within the wash sale definition and complicate the investor's tax consequences.

Investors who desire to establish ordinary losses by simultaneously purchasing and selling an identical call in opening transactions should take care. Current rulings regarding call premiums as "trade or business" income for purposes of the tax on unrelated business income of exempt organizations coupled with the *Corn Products Refining* doctrine that transactions which might be capital in nature become ordinary business transactions when closely related to the conduct of a trade or business, raise the spectre that such a matching buy/sell might not permit the desired tax consequences.

Other tax regulations worthy of consideration are:

1. Income realized by a call writer either through expiration or a profitable closing transaction is defined as ordinary income which might be interpreted as being derived from a trade or business, particularly if call writing was a continuous activity. For the individual investor, the first $13,200 of this would be subject to self-employment tax. However, 30 percent of that income would qualify as earned income subject to tax at not more than a 50-percent rate. Even if it is not trade or business income, income from call premiums does not fit the definition of "net investment income" for the purpose of computing the limitation on deduction of investment interest expense.

2. For a personal holding company, call premium income is not considered personal holding company income, making call writing an attractive area to invest.

3. For tax-exempt organizations, the fact that the IRS has ruled that call premium income is unrelated business income raises the spectre of such incomes being taxed at the same rate as are taxable organizations of the same form. This means that a tax-exempt corporation is taxed at corporate rates, a tax-exempt trust such as a pension plan or profit-sharing trust is taxed at trust rates,

which is equal to the rates for married individuals filing separate returns. However, an exempt trust should be able to reduce its tax rate from the maximum of 70 percent to the maximum corporate rate of 48 percent by setting up a feeder corporation to execute the writing of calls for the trust's stock holdings.

4. Regulated investment companies are faced with the IRS ruling that call premium income must be treated as other than dividends, interest, or gains from the sale or disposition of securities. As such under the Investment Company Act of 1940, call premium income cannot exceed 10 percent of gross income without jeopardizing the ability of the investment company to pass income tax-free to its stockholders.

5. At present there is no published IRS position regarding the characterization of call premium income for nonresident aliens or foreign corporations. The possibilities include taxation at 30 percent withheld at source, taxation at rates applicable to U.S. citizens and corporations, or complete exemption.

MARGIN REGULATIONS

Margin regulations are uniform for all fungible options, whether they are the CBOE or NOCC[1] variety.

Purchased calls must be paid for in full and have no loan value in a margin account. Payment must be received in one business day or

---

[1] National Options Clearing Corporation, the guarantor for American Stock Exchange Options.

the broker will take action to obtain the funds from the investor's account.

A fully hedged writing position requires no margin except that the determination of equity in the account is limited to the value at the strike prices of the calls written.

For writing uncovered calls the rules are as follows:

1. Thirty percent of the current market value of the underlying stock is required.
2. The 30-percent requirement is reduced by the amount of the call premiums collected.
3. Margin is increased or decreased by the amount the option is in or out of the money.
4. The minimum margin is $250 per contract.

The uniform margin regulations for fully hedged spread positions, in effect since February, 1975, essentially require a deposit equal to the maximum loss of the spread. The rules apply *only* if the short calls expire on or before the expiration date of the long calls and require that an equity of $2,000 exists in the margin account engaged in spreading. The formula to compute this maximum loss is essentially:

Cost of the Long Calls *Minus* Premiums Collected on the Short Calls *Plus* the Loss Incurred, if any, by Purchasing the Stock to Honor the Short Calls at the Exercise Price of the Long Calls.

RECORD KEEPING

Record keeping is the difference between a successful and an unsuccessful money manager. When it comes to money, the temptation is to hide from the facts because this is where the ego comes into play. The greatest psychological block to overcome is the admitting of a mistake, because for some reason the ability to make money in the stock market is associated with genius. Too many of us want to be a genius in the eyes of our peers. That is our downfall. There are two antidotes for this poison. One is not to let anyone know what you are doing and the other is to keep an exact record of where your positions stand. If a problem begins to arise, it should be corrected while it is a small problem. In fact, it is this day-to-day correcting which also distinguishes a successful options money manager. The essence is to work with the facts.

Quite obviously the records break down into those used to design a position, those used to monitor the position, and a summary of the results to date. Since writing naked is a rather straightforward procedure, the design approach will focus on hedged positions, especially partially hedged.

Figure 9–1 is an example of a general table that can be used to design virtually any hedged position whether fully or partially hedged. If fully hedged only one breakeven level will have to be determined, either a lower breakeven for a call-writing program or an upper breakeven for a put-writing program. The object of the table is to determine the maximum profitability of the positions as well as the breakeven level protection relative to the current price of the stock. To accomplish this, the total proceeds for delivering stock at the strike price are compared with the total purchase cost of the long stock to determine

FIGURE 9-1
Establishing the Position

DATE _____

COLUMN * WRITE * / POSITION	STOCK	OPTION	STOCK STOCK PRICE	STOCK PURCHASE COST	STOCK PROCEEDS IF EXERCISED	OPTIONS OPTION PREMIUM	OPTIONS TOTAL PREMIUMS	POSITION UPPER BREAKEVEN	POSITION LOWER BREAKEVEN
LONG	500 SHS XYZ		$75	$37,500	$40,000				
SHORT		10 CALLS XYZ JAN 80's				$300	$3000	91	69
LONG	1000 SHS ABX		$28	$28,000	$30,000				
SHORT		25 CALLS ABX JAN 30's				$150	$3750	$33\frac{3}{4}$	$24\frac{1}{4}$
		TOTALS		$65,500	$70,000		$6750		

MAXIMUM PROFITS = STOCK PROFIT (LOSS) @ EXERCISE + PREMIUMS COLLECTED

$= \$70,000 - \$65,500 + \$6750 = \$4500 + \$6750 = \$11,250$

CAPITAL REQUIRED = TOTAL PURCHASE COST – PREMIUMS COLLECTED = $65,500 - \$6,750$

$= \$58,750$

MAXIMUM PERCENT RETURN = $\dfrac{\text{MAXIMUM PROFITS}}{\text{CAPITAL REQUIRED}} = \dfrac{\$11,250}{\$58,750} \times 100 = 19.1\%$

an overall profit or loss on the stock side of the picture. This should be netted against the total premiums collected to arrive at the maximum profit potential. This can be compared to the total capital required to arrive at a percent return. By following this set of procedures the investor will have defined his risks and his rewards, as well as the capital required. He can adjust these to meet his guidelines before actually establishing the portfolio. In the example given, two positions XYZ and AZX require $58,-750 in capital without the use of minimum margin requirements. The $11,250 total profit potential between the appreciation of long stock to the strike price and the collection of premiums offers an 19.1 percent pretax return for the time period involved.

The next step is the position monitoring, and this begins with a mark to the market of each position every night. The suggested form for this purpose is probably best set up in a loose leaf binder as shown in Figure 9–2. The table is broken down into a Long section and a Short section. In the case of our partially hedged call writing portfolio the two long positions are the 500 shares of XYZ and 1,000 shares of AZX. The position price, which would be the average price in all cases, is posted next to the date column where the closing prices are logged. In this manner the current price and position price can be compared with the difference multiplied by the number of shares and recorded in the + column if a profit or − if a loss. After all entries are made, the + and − column entries are totalled downward so that an overall profit or loss

FIGURE 9–2

Marking to the Market

Positions Long	Position Price	Date *Nov. 7, 197–*	+	–
500 Shs. XYZ	75	73		$1,000 –
1,000 Shs. AZX	28	28½	$ 500 –	
Short				
10 Calls XYZ	$300	$225	$ 750 –	
25 Calls AZX	$150	$162.50		$312.50
			$1,250	$1,312.50

Net Loss = $1,250 – $1,312.50 = ($62.50)

for the entire portfolio can be computed. In this case it is a net loss of $62.50. The purpose of this exercise is to highlight profit opportunities or potential loss areas so that corrective action can be taken. The overall profits, if that is the case, should always be compared with the maximum potential as calculated in Figure 9–1. If this level is reached the profits should be taken.

The vertical dashed line to the right of the position price indicates where the form can be divided in two, with the right side used in the form of an overlay. This approach avoids rewriting the entire position every day and makes use of the ring binder by allowing a clean right-hand section to be laid over the previous day's results. When position changes are made a new complete page can be started.

Another important record to keep is a price follow-up as a means of learning how option premiums change with the underlying stock over

FIGURE 9–3
Price Follow-Up

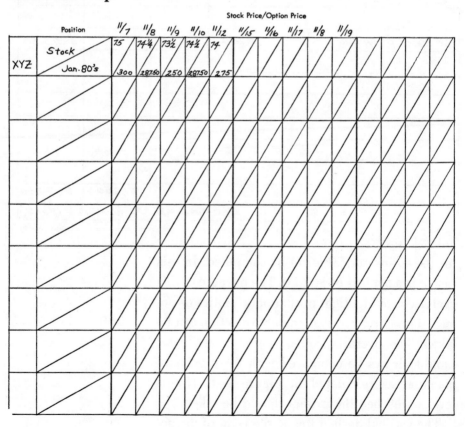

time. This is a key to developing the art of money management, because one will begin to sense how the two behave together and appreciate that if enough time has elapsed, even with the underlying stock returning to the same price, the option will lose some of its premium value, perhaps a substantial amount. Figure 9–3 offers an example of such a record.

When a position becomes involved enough to have different strike price options and different expiration dates, it is imperative that a position sheet be kept as shown in Figure 9–4. This would be especially so for a money manager handling several portfolios, because he must keep track of which portfolio or account can be affected by a particular news event or price development. He should be able to pinpoint exactly where he has to adjust. The position sheet

FIGURE 9–4
Position Sheet

XYZ

OPTIONS

Buy					Sell						
Date	Opt. Shares	Strike Price	Prem.	Exp. Date	Date	Opt. Shares	Strike Price	Prem.	Exp. Date	Profit	Loss
1/31/7X	10 CALLS	80	-0-	1/31/7X	11/7/7X	10 CALLS	80	300	1/31/7X	$3,000	

STOCK

Buy				Sell					
Date	# Shares	Price	Cost	Date	# Shares	Price	Proceeds	Profit	Loss
11/7/7X	500	75	$37,500	1/31/7X	500	79	$39,500	$2,000	

FIGURE 9–5

Summary of Realized Gains (losses)

ACCOUNT

SECURITY	AMOUNT	DATE BOUGHT	DATE SOLD	COST	PROCEEDS
XYZ CORP.	500 SHS	11/7/7X	1/31/7X	$ 37,500—	$ 39,500—
XYZ JAN 80's	10 CALLS	1/31/7X	11/7/7X	—0—	3000

should accomplish this as well as providing a summary of all closed transactions, such as that involving the XYZ Corp., which yielded an overall profit of $5,000.

The final record is a statement of profits or losses which summarizes all transactions for a given year in a fashion which provides an up-to-date tax status as the year unfolds, as well as the year-end results for income tax purposes. By use of this method the usually arduous chore of un-ravelling a year's option activity should become simplicity itself. In the case of our XYZ Corp. transactions we have a total short-term capital gain of $2,000 and total ordinary income of $3,000 (Figure 9–5).

YEAR 19___

6 SHORT-TERM		8 LONG-TERM		10 ORDINARY INCOME		12	13
GAIN	LOSS	GAIN	LOSS	GAIN	LOSS	DIVIDENDS	INTEREST
$ 2000 —							
				$ 3000 —			
$ 2000 —				$ 3000 —			

Appendix

While all evidence points to the Chicago Board type of options as the way of the future, an investor may at times desire to deal in options in non-CBOE stocks. For this reason the structure of the OTC market, how to determine option premiums, and the art of negotiating them are included in this appendix.

The traditional or over-the-counter options are contracts negotiated by a put and call broker between a buyer of an option and the guarantor of the contract, usually termed the writer. The mechanics of such a process are shown in Figure A–1. The option dealer is the core of a satellite system comprising buyers, sellers, and conversion houses. In most cases the option dealer negotiates transactions with the option department of a member firm of the New York Stock Exchange. This results from the code of business adopted in 1934, upon formation of the Put and Call Dealers Association, that all contracts are guaranteed by a NYSE member. The usual procedure is for a potential buyer of an option to ask his stock broker to purchase a call option, for example, in Xerox common stock. The usual time period is for six months and ten days so that

THE OTC OPTIONS MARKET

FIGURE A–1
The OTC Option Market

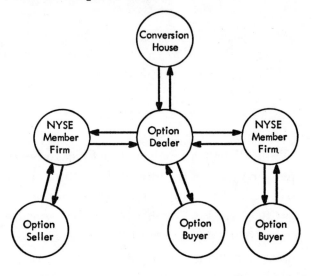

profits can be considered long term for tax purposes. The stockbroker will get in touch with
either an in-house writer of options or more
likely a put and call broker to determine whether
there are any writers interested in backing such
a contract. If the interest is found, and it should
not be difficult for such a widely held, actively
traded stock, the writer will quote a price such
as $1,450 if the stock were trading at $120 a
share. (How such a quote is arrived at will be
covered completely later in the appendix.) The
put and call broker will come back to the stockbroker through his option department with the
quote, which has been marked up slightly by the
option dealer, say to $1,500. If the customer ap-
proves, the contract will be written for that
amount at the latest market price, $120 in our
example, with the buyer charged with an addi-

tional option-writing fee of possibly $12.50 to cover the clerical work involved. The buyer is now faced with the prospect of having to make more than 15 points in Xerox during the next six months to get his money back. This is due to the $1,512.50 cost of his contract, which can only be covered if he can exercise his option, receive 100 shares of Xerox at a cost of $120 per share, and resell it for that plus $1,512.50, or $135\frac{1}{8}$ to break even. The price would actually have to be slightly more in order to cover the cost of two commissions, charged according to NYSE rules, when an option is exercised. If the stock never rose more than ten points, the option buyer could still exercise his option and at least achieve a $1,000 (less two commissions and a fee) refund on his original investment. If the stock dropped below $120 and stayed there for the entire six months and 10 days, the call would be unexercisable and the writer would pocket the $1,450 he received when the contract was written.

With this background it can be seen that the buyer's viewpoint is that Xerox will enjoy much more than a 15-point rise in price, perhaps 30 points, so that he has a chance to double his money in six months. The option writer takes the viewpoint that a 15-point rise in price is probably unlikely, no less 30 points, and besides he owns the stock, so that if it does rise that much and the call is exercised he will gladly deliver the stock, take the proceeds of $1,450 plus $12,-000 for his 100 shares at $120, buy another 100 shares and write a new option. If he is doing this with his stock he was probably thinking of selling anyway, and he has done so by making a $1,450 profit on a $12,000 investment (12 percent) in six months for a 24-percent pretax annual return. If the stock had dropped instead he would have pocketed the $1,450 premium income, still owning a stock he wants to hold long term, and write another option. In this manner an experienced option writer can earn 15 to 25 percent annual pretax return on his capital on a fairly consistent basis. While this example is a very common case, there may be many other reasons why a buyer might want to own a call option aside from outright speculation in a large price change. These were covered in the material on strategies.

The essential difference between the option buyer and the writer lies in their point of view. The buyer is willing to risk a relatively small amount of money, compared with the amount needed to own 100 shares of stock outright, for the opportunity to make a large profit during the time he owns the option. If Xerox had risen to 140 during the six-month holding period, his gross profit would have been $487.50 on $1512.50 capital, for a pretax return of 32 percent, possibly in less than six months. Although not many speculators behave in this manner (they usually hold the option for the full period), the option holder can resell his option to a dealer who will give him cash, less a small discount, for the valuable option. An alternative is to have his stockbroker exercise the option by taking delivery from the option writer of 100 shares of Xerox, paying him the $120 "strike" price of the option, and reselling the stock in the market for $140. Or, the stock purchased could be held for even higher prices.

The option writer holds the viewpoint that 20-point moves don't occur that often in a stock like Xerox, and that, rather than having to be right in forecasting such a move, he would prefer to make a more modest but consistent return on his capital. It is not necessarily that one approach is more correct than the other. It really depends on the style that is most comfortable to the individual involved. Option writing may be too dull or calculating for some, yet, to an investor seeking a relatively assured return, twice the amount of a savings account, buying an option for a large price change is a sheer gamble. The writer demands more certainty.

Who makes more money over time? That answer is not entirely clear. As Leo Pomerance will attest, any strategy adhered to rigidly for a long enough period will eventually lose an investor's capital. The answer seems to lie in adapting to the current stock market environment. For example, some accomplished traders will regularly make money buying put options in a bear market, while some writers lose a great deal of money writing calls naked (without being long the underlying stock).

Getting back to the diagram in Figure A–1 for a moment, we have not covered two elements, the option buyer who deals directly with an option dealer and the conversion house. Some active option buyers find that having an account directly with an option dealer is the most sensible way to transact their business. In most cases they don't exercise successful options, but rather sell them back to the dealer for cash. Since this is instantly credited to their account, they have the proceeds available for additional trading. Such close dealing will usually provide the trader with a lot of merchandise he might not otherwise be aware of. The house brokers, seeing the trader as an active buyer, will often show him transactions such as unexpired options just cashed in that he might want to buy for the time remaining. In addition, the paperwork of a NYSE firm having to deliver the trader's options to the dealer when cashing in, a bothersome task to some NYSE members, is avoided, along with potential accounting foul-ups by a member firm who may not emphasize option activities.

The conversion house is the banker for the over-the-counter option system, converting put options to calls or the reverse. The conversion process is necessary to counter the imbalance in the option business that is due to the phenomenon that the great majority, roughly 70 to 80 percent, of option buyers buy calls, not puts. This seems to be a parallel example of the reluctance on the part of traders in regular common stock to sell short.[1] For some reason most people approach the stock market with hope, not despair, and find it more natural to think of prospects improving, not deteriorating. This natural shortage of puts is a problem for the option

---

[1] Selling short or reverse buying is a process of selling borrowed stock immediately, it is hoped at a high price, and buying (covering short) later at a lower price to return the borrowed stock.

dealers who have many clients interested in writing straddles (a combination of a put and a call in the same stock with the same strike price and expiration date) and not enough buyers for all the puts they create. The conversion house purchases puts in exchange for calls, as well as converting calls to puts if requested. The conversion process is done risk-free and profitably. To convert a put to a call, the conversion house purchases the put, sells a call with the same strike price and expiration date and purchases 100 shares of the underlying stock. In this manner the house has protected the call obligation by fully hedging the call commitment assumed. If the stock rises in price, the gain in the 100 shares of stock is offset by the increase in the call obligation. On a fall in price, the put owned gains in value what the stock position loses. To convert a call to a put the conversion house buys the call, sells short 100 shares of the underlying stock and sells the desired put. The same principle holds of ending up with a fully hedged position, now a put obligation that is protected by a short stock position. If the stock price rises, the call owned offsets the loss in the shorted stock.

The profit made from the conversion process stems from several sources, the major one being the fee received to more than cover normal interest charges for the purchase of stock when converting a put, or the shorting of stock when converting a call. This is just compensation for the capital required in the conversion process. The conversion house also charges a nominal "floor" brokerage or paperwork fee as well as a

fee for taxes incurred. If call options converted
are exercised early, the house keeps the interest
fee for the entire period. In addition, if the calls
are exercised and the stock later drops in price,
the puts held by the house become valuable and
can be exercised for a profit.

**NEGOTIATING
PREMIUMS**

Negotiating premiums is the key to a successful operation in over-the-counter options.

Naturally, a writer of options wants to receive
as much as he can for the options he guarantees,
while the buyer wants as low a premium as possible in order to make it easier to gain a profit
on a relatively small stock price change. Contrary to some beliefs, there are no magic formulas or computerized methods used by the over-
the-counter brokers to price options. A new
trader usually spends six months in apprentice-
ship learning how to correctly quote options in
many different types of securities and for different time periods. The process is essentially one of
properly compensating a writer for the price
volatility risk he encounters in his operation. If
a premium is too small and a stock suffers a
sharp drop, a call writer can suffer a large loss
on the stock he holds while guaranteeing the option. With a fatter premium, his risk of such a
loss is decreased.

There are six factors generally considered by
a dealer in pricing an option. They are the dividend paid on the common stock (which goes to
the buyer of an over-the-counter call upon exercising), the Standard & Poor rating of the stock,
whether A, B, or C, the price/earnings ratio, the
availability of option contracts for a given stock,

the number of shares outstanding, and the fundamental outlook for the company involved.

Probably the simplest way to organize these
variables is through the scoring system detailed
in Table A–1. The logic is that anything which
increases the writer's risk of holding 100 shares
of stock to guarantee the call must be compen-
sated for through a higher premium. If a reason-

TABLE A–1

Pricing a Six Month OTC Call
(base premium for six month call = 5%)

	Factor	*Scoring*
1.	Dividend..................	Add ½ of annual yield to base premium, i.e., if dividend yield = 6%, divide by 2, = 3%. Add to 5% base = 8%
2.	S & P rating...............	A rating—no change in base B rating—add 3% to base C rating—add 6% to base No rating—add 8% to the base
3.	P/E......................	0–10—no change in base 11–20—add 1% to the base 21–40—add 3% to the base 41–60—add 5% to the base 61 + —add 7% to the base
4.	Option availability..........	Frequently quoted—no change in base Seldom quoted—add 3% to base Have to search hard for a writer—add 6% to base
5.	Shares outstanding..........	100,000 to 2 million shares—add 5% to base 2.1 million to 25 million shares—add 2% to base 26 million shares plus—no change in base

6.	Fundamental outlook........	Positive—no change in base
		Negative
		  a). Disappointing earnings—add 2% to base
		  b). Serious threat to future earnings—add 5% to base

able premium is desired for a six-month ten-day call on American Telephone the stock's risk profile in Table A–1 must be checked as follows:

AT & T Risk Profile	Score (percent)
1. Dividend yield/2 = 6.1%/2 = 3%..........................	+3
2. S & P rating = A+..	0
3. P/E (price/prior 12 months earnings) = 10.................	0
4. Option availability = most active option written............	0
5. Shares outstanding = 554 million.........................	0
6. Fundamental outlook = positive...........................	0

$$\text{Score} = 5\% \text{ base} + 3\% = 8.5\%$$
$$\text{Actual Market Quote} = 7.5\%$$
$$(3\tfrac{3}{4} \text{ on a stock price of 50})$$

The General Motors risk profile in the midst of gasoline shortages, an energy crisis, and a 30-percent drop in the sales of large cars looked like this:

General Motors Risk Profile*	Score (percent)
1. Dividend yield/2 = 10.2/2 = 5%..........................	+5
2. S & P rating = A−..	0
3. P/E (price/prior 12 months' earnings) = 5.................	0
4. Option availability = frequently quoted....................	0
5. Shares outstanding = 286 million shares....................	0
6. Fundamental outlook = market concerned with cloudy future earnings...	+2

* Note-all these statistics are available in Standard & Poor's Security Owners Stock Guide, obtainable from any stock broker.

$$\text{Score} = 5\% \text{ base} + 5\% + 2\% = 12\%$$
$$\text{Actual market quote} = 11.1\%$$
$$(5\tfrac{3}{4} \text{ on a stock price of } 51\tfrac{5}{8}$$

Natomas' risk profile at a time when the Indonesian government threatened to up its participation in oil company profits was as follows:

		Score (percent)
	Natomas Risk Profile	
1.	Dividend yield/2 = 0.4%/2 = 0.2% = 0....................	+0
2.	S & P rating = B...	+3
3.	P/E (prior 12 months' earnings) = 51 3/4/.68 = 76..........	+7
4.	Option availability = frequently quoted.....................	0
5.	Shares outstanding = 4 million shares......................	+2
6.	Fundamental outlook = market concerned with serious threat to future earnings......................................	+5

Natomas Score = 5% base + 17% = 22%
Actual Market Quote = 12¼ on a stock
  price of 51¾ = 23.7%

For Syntex, a drug stock coming back into favor after a disappointing loss of a major supply contract, the profile looked like this:

		Score (percent)
	Syntex Risk Profile	
1.	Dividend yield/2 = 0.7/2 = 0.35% = .5%.................	+½
2.	S & P rating = B+.......................................	+3
3.	P/E (price/prior 12 months' earnings) = 50 3/8/1.62 = 31...	+3
4.	Option availability = frequently quoted.....................	0
5.	Shares outstanding = 20 million shares......................	+2
6.	Fundamental outlook = market concerned with recent drop in earnings plus government investigation of drug prices......	+5

Score = 5% base + 13.5% = 18.5%
Actual quote = 10¾ on a stock price of
50⅜ = 21.3%, indicating an expensive
option.

For four very different companies the scoring method was extremely close to the actual market quote and in two cases slightly lower than the market. This is helpful for negotiating purposes because it will prevent a buyer from paying too high a price for his options. The only subjective aspects of the scoring system are option availability and fundamental outlook. A good broker should know whether options are readily available or not, but the buyer should know that most well known blue chip stocks such as American Telephone or General Motors are very popular, as are the five or so current trading favorites. The fundamental outlook can be checked with a broker, who will say things look positive or the market is concerned about the recent government anti-trust suit, etc. If the buyer finds it difficult to agree with the severity of the current fundamental outlook, he can try to buy the option at a price reflecting his outlook or simply pay up. Armed with his scoring method he has at the least a basis for making a judgment.

What about call options with maturities other than six months and ten days, or puts? The simple rule to remember is that all call options are priced relative to the six-month ten-day time period. The rules of thumb are generally as follows:

TABLE A–2

Pricing OTC Calls for Different Time Periods

Time Period	Premium Rule
30 days	$\frac{1}{2}X - \frac{1}{20}X$
60 days	$\frac{1}{2}X$
90 days	$\frac{2}{3}X$
6 month 10 day	X
1 year	$1.5X$

Here is an example using the General Motors 6 month 10 day call option with a stock price of $51\frac{5}{8}$ and a premium of $5\frac{3}{4}$.

TABLE A–3
A Sample Pricing Exercise

Time Period	Option Premium
30 days	$\frac{1}{2}X - \frac{1}{20}X = 287.50 - 28.75 = 258.75 = 2\frac{5}{8}$
60 days	$\frac{1}{2}X = 575 \div 2 = 287.50 = 2\frac{7}{8}$
90 days	$\frac{2}{3}X = 0.67$ times $\$575 = 385.25 = 3\frac{7}{8}$
6 month 10 day	$\$575 = X$
1 year	$1.5X = 1.5$ times $\$575 = \$862.50 = 8\frac{5}{8}$

Notice that the final quotes in Table A–3 are rounded up to the nearest stock type quote in terms of eighths. The 30-day call ends up as $2\frac{5}{8}$ or 262.50 rather than 258.75, the reason for this convention being that it is easy to relate the option cost to the amount of price movement needed by the call buyer to make a profit. For the 30-day call the quote of $2\frac{5}{8}$ would tell him that he needs at least that much of a rise in the price of General Motors during the next 30 days, or $51\frac{5}{8} + 2\frac{5}{8} = 54\frac{1}{4}$ to break even on his call cost. Of course this doesn't include the two commissions he would be charged to exercise his call.

For time periods differing from the usual ones found in Table A–3, the square root rule can be applied. Again the six-month ten-day option is used as the benchmark. If a $1\frac{1}{2}$ month option were to be priced the time period of roughly 45 days would be divided by 190 days for the six-month ten-day option to obtain a ratio of 45/190 or 0.237. The square root of 0.237 is 0.487 which when multiplied times the $575 premium for the standard option yields $280 or $2\frac{7}{8}$ according to stock market quotes. As we will see later, our quoting methods are guides to assist in negotiating a fair premium, not an unbendable rule.

Puts are quoted differently and can vary much more widely than call quotes for a given stock. The reason for this is that there is usually an excess supply of puts available compared to the demand for them. As mentioned before, puts are the byproduct of writing straddles, the combination of a put and a call, which most option writers prefer because they can earn a greater return for the capital they have tied up in the 100 shares of stock guaranteeing the option. If the stock involved is a frequently written one such as American Telephone, the put premium is considered gravy by the writer and he is willing to settle for a lower than usual premium just to get the added income. In general, the roughest rule of thumb is that a put premium is 45/55 of the corresponding call premium. For our six-month ten-day General Motors call, the $575 premium would be reduced by 45/55 times $575 or $4\frac{3}{4}$ for the put. Another rule is the premium of the call minus the stock price or $575 - 51\frac{5}{8} =$ $5\frac{1}{4}$ for an inactively written stock or the call premium minus two times the stock price or $575 - \$103.25 = 4\frac{3}{4}$, matching the 45/55 quote. For a put buyer it is probably simplest to use the 45/55 rule and then determine from your broker whether the put is easy or difficult to obtain. If easy you may be able to shade the premium in your favor. If not, you may have to pay slightly more than 45/55ths.

Is there a link between OTC and CBOE options? The simple answer is that the CBOE provides such an excellent market for writers and buyers to deal with each other that, whenever a new stock is added to the CBOE roster, the OTC market for that call option dies. In addition, the writers of CBOE calls obtain all dividends, in the OTC market they don't; therefore, why write OTC calls? The interesting phenomenon is that while the CBOE does not offer puts, OTC put premiums for stocks written on the CBOE generally have higher quotes than the CBOE calls. The difference is usually 10 to 15 percent of the CBOE call premium.

Which brings us back to the purpose of determining fair quotes, the ability to negotiate your premiums in the OTC market.

A typical conversation between you and your broker might go something like this:

YOU: Hi, Jim. George here. What are you quoting six-month calls on Natomas?

YOUR BROKER: Let me check. (pause) I think I can get several for you at 12½; the current stock price is 51¾. How many do you want?

YOU: Probably no more than five. But isn't that a little high? Let me see, at 51¾ my calculations come up with about 10⅜ (using the scoring method and a moderately negative fundamental outlook).

YOUR BROKER: Never!

You: Why?

Your broker: Haven't you heard about the Indonesian government threatening to change their tax rules? They want a much bigger participation. Just like the Arabs.

You: No kidding (rechecking your fundamental factor and raising it to 5%). What if I buy ten?

Your broker: Let me see what I can do. Hold on. (pause) OK. I found a writer of ten who will take 12¼ for all ten.

You: That still sounds high (your own score now says 12¼ is fair, but for a larger quantity you want somewhat of a break). I'll pay 12 flat. Take it or leave it!

Your broker: Just a second. (pause) OK. He'll do it for 12. But only if you do all ten.

You: Done.

Your broker: OK, it's yours. Ten six-month calls at 12. Let me see what Natomas is trading at now. OK, 51⅞. That's your strike.

You: OK, George.

Your broker: Do you want me to call you if I find any more?

You: No thanks. That should hold me for now. Thanks a lot, George. I'll talk to you later.

Your broker: So long.

The reader might ask, "Why do I have to know anything about the over-the-counter market if the Chicago Board Options Exchange is so popular?" The answer is that there are still many uses for the over-the-counter market, the main one being that Chicago Board options were only traded for 32 major blue chip companies as of June 1, 1974. If a holder of stocks outside this list wants to write calls or a speculator wants to capitalize on a stock price change in an issue away from the CBOE he has to trade in OTC options. However, as the record to date indicates, the many superior features of CBOE options have drawn a great deal of activity away from the over-the-counter market.

Index